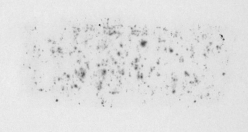

THE HOPE OF THE AGES

The Hope of the Ages

THE MESSIANIC HOPE IN REVELATION, IN HISTORY AND IN REALIZATION

BY

ARNO CLEMENS GAEBELEIN, D.D.

Editor of "Our Hope"; Author of the
"Annotated Bible"; and many volumes
of Biblical Research and Exposition

PUBLICATION OFFICE "OUR HOPE"
(Arno C. Gaebelein, Inc.)
456 Fourth Avenue, New York, N. Y.

PICKERING & INGLIS 14 Paternoster Row London, E. C. Glasgow, Scotland H. L. THATCHER 135 Symonds Street Auckland, N. Z.	G. E. ARDILL 145 Commonwealth Street Sydney, N. S. W. KESWICK BOOK DEPOT 315 Collins Street Melbourne, Australia *All Booksellers in U. S. A.*

Dedicated

To my beloved friends of many years,
MR. AND MRS. SIDNEY T. SMITH
OF WINNIPEG, MANITOBA; and to
ELIM CHAPEL, in deep appreciation
of their loyalty to the Lord Jesus
Christ and the work of the Gospel.

Foreword

The completion of Dr. Gaebelein's book, **The Hope of the Ages,** has been awaited with keen interest. For many generations the Church has sorely needed this treatise and there is no one who combines the requisite essentials to the authorship of such an authoritative declaration—knowledge of Church History in its far-flung issues; knowledge of books in general and of the Word of God in particular including that grasp of divine prediction which is gained only by a life-time of unrelenting, scholarly study; and a masterful understanding of world governments and the problems they engender—as does Dr. Gaebelein. An advance reading of this book having been accorded me, I state with genuine enthusiasm that it has proven to be to me illuminating, convincing, confirming, and heartening. Forty years of research along lines of Bible truth has not only provided a perspective which enables me to see the surpassing value of the work Dr. Gaebelein has done, but leads me to some definite convictions:

It is both fortunate and unfortunate that the vast majority of people read only the literature which sustains their preconceived ideas—fortunate in so far as it retards the spreading of untruth, and unfortunate when it retards the spreading of truth. Within the church a division has arisen which is present in all denominations, separating men within a denomination by a greater distance than men have ever been divided over denominational tenets. One class is liberal and reads only the literature which is liberal and negative; the other class is conservative and reads largely the literature which is conservative and constructive. Even men who claim to be sound as to the inspiration of the Scriptures, the virgin birth, the Deity of Christ, and redemption by blood alone, are so divided as to their eschatological views that they attend but little on the teachings of those with whom they disagree; though it must be said that the post and amillennialists have created practically no literature on these themes, and that the premillennialists have usually read with care such literature as their opponents have produced. That this literature is thus read is demonstrated by the fact that the premillennialist is able to state the position and belief of his opponent as precisely as the authors themselves; whereas evidence is given that these authors do not read the premillennial literature by the fact that any attempt these authors make to state the premillennial position and belief would be ludicrous were it not so serious. Little do these authors realize the spectacle they create when venturing into that great field of truth which can be included only in the premillennial interpretation. When it comes to prophecy and all it comprehends, the post and amillennial writers may be classed as the **leave-it-alones,** while the premillennial teachers are tireless in their pursuance of eschatological truth.

The future aspect of any doctrine is usually its most determining feature. This is as true of redemption as it is of resurrection, and, without a clear apprehension of its consummation, all the rest of a doctrine is not only incomplete but is distorted. God's revealed truth is a system which is as dependent on the functioning of all its parts as is His creation. It is not an overstatement to declare that revealed truth suffers as much or more from neglect or distortion of one of its parts as does the human body when a vital organ is diseased or removed altogether. The term **theologian** has been applied to men who construct apologetics in a restricted field of truth; but these men seldom undertake Scripture exposition. More consideration would be accorded them if they presented some workable interpretation of such great passages as Deuteronomy, chapter 30; the Davidic Covenant; the Second Psalm; the prophetic portions of the prophetic books; the Olivet Discourse; Acts, chapter 15; Romans, chapters 9-11; 1 Corinthians, chapter 15; the Thessalonian letters; the letters to Timothy; James, chapter 5; 2 Peter; Jude; and the unsearchable treasures of eschatology which are the warp and woof of the Revelation. Much is made in America of Bible exposition and a class of men who are grounded in unabridged Systematic Theology and who have specialized in the knowledge of the Scriptures has arisen who are styled **Bible Teachers,** and these are premillennial without exception. Dr. Gaebelein has faithfully pointed out that the ministry of premillennial evangelists, pastors, and teachers is effective to a manifest degree, if notice is taken of the multitudes who attend upon their ministry, the souls saved, and the advancement to missionary enterprise. This effectiveness can be explained only on the ground of the truth that it is Spirit-empowered. It is suggestive to note in this connection that the first theme which Christ declared the Spirit would teach those who are subject to Him is "things to come." And what is to be implied concerning theologians who ignore future things?

As the Arminian is not Pauline in his theology when he says, "I am **not** persuaded that Christ is able to guard my deposit against that day," so the theologian is not Pauline when he omits from his teaching the themes of prediction. It is demonstrated that Paul taught the most advanced prophetic truth to his young converts. He was in Thessalonica less than five weeks. In that time the people were saved who formed that local church and the Apostle had taught them enough to make it possible for him to write both letters to them, after he was driven away from their city. Having made reference to great themes of prediction, he goes on to say, "Remember ye not that I told you these things while I was yet with you?" So, also, he declared regarding prophecy, "These things speak"; and in another place he asserts that he would himself win the title of "a good soldier of Jesus Christ" by putting the brethren in remembrance of certain vital aspects of prophecy. From all this it may be concluded that to neglect prophetic truth is to depart from the teachings and injunctions of the great Apostle. A word of criticism of other men would be withheld if it were a personal matter, but literally millions are being misled by guides who are themselves apparently blind. The **liberty** to delete one feature of truth, which is the custom of some who claim to be sound in the faith, has given others a **license** to delete every vital thing, and the question is in order as to who is the instigator of modernism with all its blasting effects.

This volume demands consideration of all sincere Christians. It will establish those who know something of God's program and will be a corrective to those who, for want of personal study, are trafficking in borrowed opinions. The proof Dr. Gaebelein adduces that Chiliasm has been the true doctrine of the church in all generations is conclusive, and every theologian who is of a contrary mind is challenged to read and be admonished by this masterful and indisputable treatise.

If I could say but three words in my foreword to this volume, I would say, **Read this book.** If I could say but twenty-one words I would only repeat those three words seven times. I thank God for the author, and for the great book he has written.

LEWIS SPERRY CHAFER.

Dallas, Texas.

TABLE OF CONTENTS

Foreword by Lewis S. Chafer, D. D.

PART I

The Hope in Revelation: fulfilled and unfulfilled

PART II

The Hope in History
From Apostolic Days to Our Times
The Approaching Realization

PART I
THE HOPE IN REVELATION

The Hope of the Ages

CHAPTER I

When Hope Was Born

The great eulogy of love, penned by the Apostle Paul in his first Epistle to the Corinthians, has charmed and inspired the minds and hearts of countless thousands in every generation. How deep and how searching are these terse aphorisms, beloved by all Christian believers! "Love suffereth long, and is kind; love envieth not; love vaunteth not itself, is not puffed up, doth not behave itself unseemly, seeketh not her own, is not easily provoked, thinketh no evil; rejoiceth not in iniquity, but rejoiceth in the truth; beareth all things, believeth all things, hopeth all things, endureth all things. Love never faileth" (1 Cor. xiii:4-8). At the close of this chapter faith, hope and love are mentioned. "And now abideth faith, hope, love, these three; but the greatest of these is love."

And why is love so great? Why is love greater than faith and hope? Why is it the greatest thing, towering above everything else? Because, *God is Love.* Some have imagined that God became Love. God never became anything. What God is He has always been, and what God has been He always will be. God is Love and therefore Love is eternal. Faith and hope had their beginning in time. Neither of them is eternal. Faith and hope will some day pass away; they will cease. Love never! For God is Love.

An eternal Being of eternal Light, eternal Life, eternal Love! A Being of eternal Power, eternal Omniscience, eternal Righteousness, eternal Holiness, eternal Goodness and Mercy! It staggers our human brain! It transcends all human reason, yet it is far from being unreasonable. Atheism is unreasonable. The denial of an intelligent Creator is unreasonable. So is the theory that life created itself and that all originated by chance. An eternal Being of infinite power and wisdom alone is the solution of the great riddle of the universe.

Several years ago I overheard the conversation of a mother with her inquisitive child. The child in seeing from the railroad train tanks filled with gas was curious to know where the gas comes from. The mother explained that it comes from coal. The next question was, where does coal come from? The mother replied that coal is taken from deep mines. "Well, mother," continued the youngster, "how did coal get to be so far down in the earth?" Sweetly the mother gave the information that God had made this provision so that people can get coal to heat their houses, and also gas to give them light. After a brief pause there came another question which exhausted the good woman's patience, and she answered in anything but sweet tones, and commanded the little one to keep her mouth shut after that. The question was, "Mother, where does God come from?"

The Bible is the only book in the world which gives a satisfactory and a satisfying revelation of the higher Being, the eternal and almighty God. Nothing so sublime as the words, written in a few sentences by that great man of God, Moses, appears anywhere in the religious-philosophical writings of the East—"Before the mountains were brought forth, or ever Thou hadst formed the earth and the world, even from everlasting to everlasting, Thou art God" (Psa. xc:2). Nor is this the only great utterance about the Eternal One. The Bible abounds in many such majestic statements as to God and His attributes and His glory. But nowhere do we find even a hint which sheds any light whatever on the mystery of His self-existence, as the Being who had no beginning. And so we say it again, God and His eternal Being transcends our finite reason. *God is Love*. But how can love be manifested without a person or an object? Did God in His solitary eternity love? Before the earth and the universe existed how did He express His love? There is an answer to this question. The author of the Book of books, the Bible, the Spirit of God, through human penmen, tells us of One whom God loved, upon whom His eternal love rested and still rests. We read of that One as, "the Only Begotten Son, which is in the bosom of the Father" (John i:18). He is called "the Son of His Love" (Col. i:13; Greek text). Nor is this truth of the eternal existence of the Son of God confined to the writings of the New Testament. Solomon, the King of Israel, in his inspired Proverbs glorifies wisdom. But it is more than wisdom; wisdom is personified, even as the New Testament reveals that the Son of God is the Wisdom of God. Of Him Solomon speaks.

"The Lord possessed Me in the beginning of His way, before His works of old. I was set up from everlasting, from the beginning, or ever the earth was. When there were no depths, I was brought forth; when there were no fountains abounding with water. Before the mountains were settled, before the hills was I brought forth; while as yet He had not yet made the earth, nor the fields, nor the highest part of the dust of the world. When He prepared the heavens, I was there; when He set a compass upon the face of the depth; when He established the clouds above; when He strengthened the fountains of the deep; when He gave to the sea His degree, that the waters should not pass His commandment; when He appointed the foundations of the earth, then I was by Him, as one brought up with Him; and I was daily His delight, rejoicing always before Him" (Prov. viii:22-30).

It is a beautiful description, adapted to our finite minds, of Him whose eternal resting place was the bosom of the Father.

We might quote next the statements of great theological thinkers, beginning with the noble church-fathers, and continue through the Middle Ages and the subsequent Reformation periods, listening to their attempts to explain in some way the person of the "Only Begotten" and His eternal existence. We could also turn to different creedal expressions and confessions such as the Nicene, the Athanasian and others. If we did we would have to confess, after examining these explanations and definitions, that the person of the "Only Begotten" still remains unsolved. We would have to step on the territory of philosophical speculation and land as a result in the fogs of doubt and questionings.

"Why do you think there has been so much doubt about and so many opinions as to the person of our Lord, His relation to the Father, and so many unscriptural teachings," some one inquired. The sources are the well-meant attempts of finite men to explore, to define and to fathom the infinite. The better way is to accept the plain statements of the Scriptures in faith, with the acknowledgment, though humiliating, that it is all beyond our ken. "Canst thou by searching find out God?" is an old, patriarchial question (Job ii:7). Let a philosopher like Lessing, and many others, in pride of intellect answer in the affirmative and claim that searching, scientific knowledge will ultimately solve all mysteries. True Christian believers, including many master-minds, acknowledge their human limitations, and trusting in the divine revelation of God's holy Word, bow in faith before its declarations.

We as believers accept therefore the plain statement which came from the lips of the Son of God in incarnation, "No man knoweth the Son, but the Father" (Matt. ii:27).

But we have additional information from the Word of God. The "Only Begotten," the eternal object of the Father's Love is according to divine revelation the One by whom and for whom God created all things. We call attention to the following Scripture passages without explaining them: John i:1-5, 10; Colossians i:15-17; Hebrews i:1-3. In the light of these statements, not the products of human research, but of divine revelation, we are authorized to say that God creating by the Son of His love and for Him, expressed in this way His love for the Only Begotten. Creation therefore is, besides a manifestation of the almighty power of God, a manifestation of His love.

Among all the things created by and for the Son of God are the invisible things—thrones, dominions, principalities and powers. This is the great unseen world of spirit beings above. That such a world of spirits exists is fully demonstrated in almost every portion of the Bible. The existence of such unseen spirits, is likewise the traditional and mythological belief of all nations. Lately even certain scientists have expressed their opinion that intelligent beings exist elsewhere in this great universe.* While these unseen spirits, the angels of God, are prominent on many pages of sacred history, and a future glorious manifestation of their hosts is promised, we again must confess that we know but little of that great world above, for we are only looking into a glass darkly. But this is certain they were created for God's pleasure (Rev. v:11). They are another evidence that God is Love. In what a remote past these beings of glory were created we do not know. Scripture is silent and no searching will lift the veil.

Let us listen next to an outburst of praise which came from the lips of David, the Shepherd-king. "When I consider Thy heavens, the work of Thy fingers, the moon and the stars, which Thou hast ordained; what is man that Thou art mindful of him? and the son of man, that Thou visitest him? For Thou hast made him a little lower than the angels, and hast crowned him with glory and honor" (Psa. viii:3-5).

This interesting Scripture looks backward and forward. It reveals man's noble origin, the glory of the first man; it also makes known the glory of the second Man, the last Adam. (See Heb. ii:5-9). We are now concerned with the head of the human race, the first man. The Darwinian evolution-invention has been completely pushed aside by modern scientific research. It is no longer held by real scholarly scientists. Many of them begin to believe in a direct creatorship and abandon spontaneous creation. If man were an evolved beast with beastly instincts, vicious and degrading, man would not be the product of a God of love. Such a creature would be a discredit to God. Man *became* beastly.

The great truth, which can never be shaken by science, that truth which crowns man's creation with glory and honor, which confers upon him a majestic nobility, was

---

*See the author's work, "The Angels of God."

written by the inspired pen of Moses, at a time when other
pens wrote their cosmogonies in a ridiculous babble, which
taxes the credulity of the mind of man.

"And God said, Let us make man in our own image,
after our likeness; and let them have dominion over the
fish of the sea, and over the fowl of the air, and over the
cattle, and over all the earth, and over every creeping thing
that creepeth upon the earth. So God created man in
His image, in the image of God created He him; male and
female created He them" (Gen. i:26, 27). It was again a
manifestation of "God is Love." Man is the offspring of
God, made a little lower than the angels. Then He crowned
His condescending love by giving to man the woman,*
bone of his bone, and flesh of his flesh, and assigned to them
an earthly paradise, the garden of Eden. Such an original
dwelling place of man, a home of joy and glory, undisturbed
by anything evil, lives, in a distorted way, in the traditions
and mythologies of all nations.

How often we have enjoyed a charming landscape, the
towering mountains, the peaceful meadows, the quiet and
restful forest, the babbling mountain brook, and praised
the heavenly Father for all His works, called into existence
for His pleasure, which His child can share. Then came
the thought of storms and floods, cyclones and tornadoes,
sweeping over all, uprooting the monarchs of the forest,
spreading devastation in every direction. We thought
of earthquakes and volcanic disturbances. We thought of
the garden of Eden, that earthly Paradise, man's blessed
home. We thought how indescribably wonderful it must
have been. What homage the beasts of the forests must
have paid to that first pair! How lions and tigers, peace-
fully purring, crouched at their feet! All physical need was
supplied. There was no struggle for existence. Disease,
pain and death were unknown. Above all there was supreme

---

*It is not a second account of creation, added by a later hand, as
Bible critics claim, which we find in the second chapter of the Bible
concerning the formation of the woman out of Adam's side. The
details of man's creation are revealed by the Spirit of God.

happiness, supreme delight, supreme glory in the blessed fellowship they enjoyed with the Lord God their Creator, the God of Love.

What a day it must have been when the gates of Paradise, that earthly restful home, which knew no want, opened outwardly! What an hour it must have been when these days of heaven on earth were forever ended! The record says, "Therefore the Lord God sent him forth from the garden of Eden, to till the ground from whence he was taken. So He drove out the man; and He placed at the East of the garden of Eden Cherubim, and a flaming sword which turned every way, to keep the way to the tree of life" (Gen. iii:23, 24). Why it was, why Eden was lost, why the Lord God and man were separated, our former books of this series have made plain.

Soon we see them tilling the ground. The sweat pours from Adam's brow. A year passes and thorns and thistles spring up everywhere. The great struggle has begun. Eve becomes a mother. Travail pains seize her; she cries out in physical agony. Adam stands by unable to relieve her sorrow. Man became afflicted with pain and disease. Yes, there was joy over the birth of Cain, over Abel, and over daughters as well, though the parents must have realized they all would but be sharers of their unhappy lot. Years come and go. Let us imagine what happened. One day Cain returned from the field. But where is Abel? "Cain, Cain what has become of Abel? Cain where is your brother Abel?" asks anxiously mother Eve.

With a guilty look upon his face, evading the searching eyes of his mother, Cain answers, "Am I my brother's keeper?" Go and find him yourself. Eve finds the lifeless corpse of her beloved Abel. He is dead. Death had visited for the first time the human race. How she must have wept over him!

Perhaps many a day when evening came, when the daily task was finished and Adam wiped the sweaty brow, the pair may have gone to some elevation. There they stopped. In the distance they saw perhaps a revolving light, the flaming swords of the Cherubim. With wistful eyes they looked in that direction. Regret and sorrow must have filled Eve's heart as she remembered her transgression, after having listened to the mysterious serpent. There, there is our lost Paradise, our Eden! Both must have deplored their lost inheritance. No doubt many times they longed to be back; they hoped to be back. They prayed, perhaps, that Eden's portal might open again and receive them once more. The howling wolves, the roaring lions and snarling tigers, which surrounded them now, reminded them of the peace they had lost. Oh! to be back in Paradise! Oh! to be back in His fellowship!

Yes hope, that emotion of time, had been born. It was born before they had been driven from Eden's hallowed surroundings. The Lord God had spoken. He spoke in promise. He spoke of the future. *Hope rests on faith.* Both rest upon the Word of God. Where there is no faith there can be no hope. Faith and hope were born in the garden of Eden.

What that faith and hope was and still is for the entire race, how it reveals ultimately the highest, the most glorious manifestation that "God is Love," we follow in our next chapters.

CHAPTER II

The Hope is a Person

Faith and hope were born when man sinned and fell. But before faith and hope could become man's possession God had to speak. Thousands of years later we find it written, "Faith cometh by hearing, and hearing by the Word of God" (Rom. x:17). Faith, founded upon the Word of God, generates hope. So before man could believe and hope, the Lord God had to speak. God's words are deep, inexhaustible, yet simple. This is most true of His first utterance in the dawn of human history, spoken in the glorious home of Eden. Genesis iii:15 consists in the Hebrew text of only fifteen words, yet it contains, as in a nutshell, the history of the race and above all the history of redemption. It has well been said that our first parents listening to these fifteen words, "took with them from Paradise the Magna Charta of human history; they entered into the world to engage in a life-long struggle whose issue is death and victory. From their Creator's hands they received the Protevangelium, the glad tidings of redemption." This still is true. Here is human history, human destiny and above all God's redemption, prewritten.

"And I will put enmity between thee (the serpent) and the woman, and between thy seed and her seed, it shall bruise thy head, and thou shalt bruise his heel." Marvelous! The entire history and order of redemption are announced and unfolded in these few words. It is the germ of all prophecy out of which the history of redemption develops. "Like a sphinx, it crouches at the entrance of sacred history. Later in the period of Israelitish Prophecy, the solution of this riddle of the Sphinx begins to dawn; and it is only solved by Him through whom and in whom that has been revealed towards which this primitive prophecy was aimed."* There is some truth in the claim that the term seed is a generic term for the entire race of descendants of the woman

---

*"Messianic Prophecy," by Franz Delitzsch. Page 33.

on the one hand, and the serpent on the other. Yet as far
as the woman's seed is concerned it must be applied only to
those who fall in line with God's purposes in redemption.
All others constitute the seed of the serpent, that part of
humanity which is and remains under the influence of the
liar and murderer from the beginning, the devil. This great
conflict the author has traced from its beginnings in history into our own times, when God's redemption program nears its predicted consummation, in "The Conflict
of the Ages."

We must remember that both the seed of the woman and
the seed of the serpent mean a person. This is seen by the
expressions "*thy* head" and "*his* heel," as well as by the
word *thou.*

The seed of the woman, a person, is to conquer the serpent, also a person, by crushing the head of the serpent.*
But the seed of the woman is to suffer; his heel will be
crushed. Suffering is involved in the crushing of the head
of the serpent. The conquest of the author of evil, the
serpent, will be brought about by the seed of the woman.
The seed of the woman, as we shall discover in the gradual
unfolding of this first promise and prophecy in Scripture, is
Jehovah, taking on the human body, thus becoming man,
"God manifested in the flesh," a second man.† He was
present on the scene of man's fall and ruin; yea, His own
mouth uttered the sentence of judgment and gave the first
great promise of redemption. He is the same who rested
in the bosom of God, the eternal object of God's love, by
whom and for whom God created all things. But how can
we be sure of this? What reasons have we to believe this?
Though we have stated it in previous volumes, it bears
repetition. The name of God in the first chapter of Genesis
is *Elohim*, denoting power and is in the plural, evidenced

---

*We prefer the word "crush" as it better expresses the original word.
It also corresponds to the Greek word used in Romans xvi:20.

†The Roman Catholic Church has invented the theory that the seed
means the Virgin Mary, thus sustaining her Mary idolatry.

by the "Let us" (verse 26). In the second chapter of
Genesis when God is seen in intimate fellowship with His
creature the word *Jehovah* (Yahweh) is added—Jehovah
Elohim. Upon this fact Higher Criticism has erected its
system and formulated the theory of at least two writers of
the book of Genesis, one who used the word Elohim (Elohist)
and another who used Jehovah (Jehovist). It is an exploded theory which we do not need to answer.

Jehovah—"The I Am" (Exod. iii:14), whom we know as
God the Son, whose voice of love had delighted the man and
the woman, but whose approach after their transgression
filled the guilty pair with fear and trembling (Gen. iii:8),
came into the garden to seek and to save what was lost.
He announced then His own program of redemption. Man
knew not fully what it all meant and included. Man had
to wait for the progressive revelation of God's purposes in
the written Word. But He, in His omniscience, in whom
God planned even before the foundation of the world not
only a physical creation, but a glorious redemption, knew
the end from the beginning. It is written, "By whom He
also made the worlds," which here does not mean physical
worlds, but *the ages*, the different dispensations (Heb. i:2).
Therefore when He spoke the words of hope, He knew
what it meant. When the triune God said, "Let us make
man in our own image, after our likeness," when *Jehovah-
Elohim* formed man out of the dust of the ground, and
breathed into his nostrils the breath of life, He, Jehovah the
Son, knew that some day He would clothe Himself with
such a body, and appear as the seed of the woman, that He
would come as the God-sent-One "made of a woman" (Gal.
iv:4). He knew, before the Spirit of God revealed it in the
Holy Scriptures, what would be that mysterious crushing
of the heel. He saw that Cross, its sufferings and its shame,
that Cross with its unfathomable depths, demanded by the
righteousness and holiness of God. He knew all the enmity
between the two seeds, the mighty struggles throughout the
ages. Much more than that loomed up before Him as He
spoke for the first time. He saw the ultimate victory, the

dethronement of evil, the enthronement of righteousness. From start to finish the history of redemption was before Him as an open book. All the eternal purposes of God were known to Him from the beginning for they were all made in and for Him. He is the center of them all.

We must now trace Messianic Prophecy, the great hope, in its progressive revelation, the object of faith, as revealed in the oracles of God. Several years ago a book appeared on Prophecy claiming to be "an exhaustive study." We do not make such a claim for we know God's revelation in His Word can never be exhausted. Ours is a brief review of Him who is the Hope of the Ages and an equally brief description of His great work.

Genesis iii:15 is the only Messianic Prophecy which was given to the antediluvian world. We must refer the reader to our work "As It Was—So Shall It Be," for a description of the age before the flood. The faith of Adam and Eve laid hold on the promise and hope filled their hearts. Their descendants were divided into two classes, those who believed and those who believed not. The offspring of Seth constituted the believers, the generations of hope; the offspring of Cain were the unbelievers, whose hope consisted in earthly things. Assuredly the Holy Spirit shed much light upon the first Messianic Prophecy so that the vision of hope became brighter. An Enoch, walking with God, experienced a blessed and glorious realization of his hope, when, "by faith," he "was translated that he should not see death." A ray of hope is also seen in the words of the father of Noah, Lamech. Lamech called his son Noah, which means "comfort" and said, "This same shall comfort us concerning our work and for the toil of our hands, because of the ground which Jehovah hath cursed" (Gen. v:29). It was an expression of Lamech's hope, because he believed the first promise of redemption. "The comfort which he expected through Noah is not the comfort of words, but the comfort of an act of salvation. This comfort was fulfilled through him, although not fully and completely, but in a way preparatory to the completion. The rainbow after the flood was a comfort, the blessing of which extended from that time on. It pledged mankind, after the judgment visitation, a continuance of the race, and of the dawn of better things, when instead of wrath, blessing is to predominate."* Noah is then seen as the first mediator in sacred history, a mediator of comfort. It is of interest to know that the ancient synagogical writers called frequently the promised Messiah *Menachem*—Comforter.

The second Messianic Prophecy is found in the words of Noah concerning his three sons, Shem, Ham and Japheth.

This Prophecy is recorded in Genesis ix:24-27. Curse and blessing are mentioned as in the third chapter of Genesis. Without quoting the text or explaining the incident upon which Noah uttered his prophetic words we briefly state that the divine blessing is promised to *Shem*. "And he said, Blessed be Jehovah God of Shem . . . God shall enlarge Japheth, and He shall dwell in the tents of Shem." The word "Shem" means, Name. Here is the promise that the Jehovah-God revelation is to take place in connection with Shem. He will manifest Himself in Shem. It is a question whether the word "He" means Jehovah-God or Japheth. The author has come to the conclusion that it must mean Jehovah-God; He comes to dwell in the tents of Shem and establishes a relationship there. It has also been applied to Japheth sharing the blessings of Shem. "In the former prophecy (Gen. iii:15) we have the human side of Messianic redemption brought out in the victory of the seed of the woman over the serpent. Here, on the other hand, we have the divine side of Messianic redemption in the prediction of the advent of God as a blessing in the tents of Shem. These two lines of Messianic prophecy, the human and the divine, henceforth develop side by side; they approximate at times, but never converge till they unite in the person of Jesus Christ, the God-man, at His *first advent*, and still more at His *second advent*."† The God of salvation will be the God of Shem.

---

*Franz Delitzsch: "Messianic Prophecies."

†"Messianic Prophecy," by Dr. Charles Augustus Briggs. Page 82.

For a time the sons of Noah and their families remained together. But soon came the time when they attempted in a plain in the land of Shinar, to make unto themselves a name by building a gigantic tower, an act of God defiance. They knew God but "they glorified Him not as God, neither were thankful; but became vain in their imaginations, and their foolish heart was darkened" (Rom. i:21). God executed a judgment upon them. The confusion of tongues followed. They were scattered upon the face of all the earth. Corruption followed rapidly. Faith in Jehovah-God was given up. Idolatry took its place and indescribable immoralities appeared everywhere. The hope of redemption was either completely abandoned or became distorted.

Several centuries passed when suddenly God acted in the execution of His redemptive purposes. While the descendants of Ham and Japheth scattered in various directions, thus becoming the progenitors of the different nations, so correctly traced in the tenth chapter of Genesis, the offspring of Shem remained close to the cradle land of the human race. In the eleventh chapter of Genesis (verses 10-32) we find the generations of Shem. Prominent among these are Terah and his three sons, Abram, Nahor, and Haran. Their home was Ur in Chaldea. Idolatry flourished everywhere, confirmed by the excavations carried on by archaeologists, who have unearthed large numbers of votive objects used in a perverted worship. This is confirmed by the Bible, for we read that Joshua said, "Thus saith the Lord God of Israel, Your fathers dwelt on the other side of the flood in old time, even Terah the father of Abraham, and the father of Nahor, and they served other gods" (Josh. xxiv:2). The whole family were idolators.

A memorable day it was when the voice of Jehovah was

Over fifty years ago Dr. Briggs taught in the Union Theological Seminary of New York City. He was known as a higher critic. He was far from being a *destructive critic*. We shall quote him again to show his faith in prophecy, in the Deity of our Lord in His Virgin birth and in the Cross. No Modernist accepts today his scholarly testimony. It shows the progress of the apostasy.

heard again. In sovereign grace He selected the oldest son of Terah, Abram. The communication was connected with a supernatural manifestation. Stephen spoke of this when he addressed the Sanhedrin in that remarkable testimony which resulted in his martyr's death. "The God of glory appeared unto our father Abraham, when he was in Mesopotamia, before he dwelt in Charran" (Acts vii:2). We do not know in what form the God of glory appeared unto this Semite. Perhaps He came, as He so often did afterwards, in the form of an angel, the *Malach Jehovah*, the Angel of the Lord. His first message to Abram was the message of separation. He was called upon to leave his own country, to turn his back upon the land of idolatry and to go to another land which Jehovah would show him. Linked with the call to separation are unconditional promises. It is not the purpose of this volume to follow the different promises in the beginning of Abram's call, nor to follow their interesting expansion, culminating in a covenant. The promises speak of great blessings, national greatness, the possession of a great territory, far greater than the little coast land of today called Palestine (Gen. xv:18-20). One word is prominent in all these promises, in fact it is the very heart of the entire Abrahamic covenant. It is the word "seed." It is used twenty-four times in the biography of Abraham the friend of God. Abraham's seed is to be like the dust of the earth and like the stars of heaven, an earthly and a heavenly seed. Yet the seed of Abraham has a far deeper meaning. The Epistle to the Galatians, gives us the key. Jehovah had promised to Abraham that in him all nations were to be blessed. Here is the Pauline comment: "And the Scripture, foreseeing that God would justify the Gentiles through faith, preached before the Gospel unto Abraham, saying, In thee shall all nations be blessed" (Gal. iv:8). But how? In his seed. But who is that seed? We listen again to the witness of God's Spirit through Paul. "Now to Abraham and his seed were the promises made. He saith not, And to seeds, as of many; but as of one, And to thy seed, *which is Christ*" (Gal. iv:16). The word "seed" in whom and through whom the nations are to receive blessing has therefore the same meaning as in Genesis iii:15, the seed of the woman. We notice then in the promise of Hope, the Person who is the Hope, a narrowing revelation. First, the seed is to be of the *woman*; then narrower, that seed is to be not of Ham or Japheth, but of the *race* of Shem and still narrower, he will be Abraham's seed. The promise of the seed, as we shall see directly, is again narrowed to a certain tribe and to a certain family of that tribe.

Three times Abraham received the promise that all the kindreds of the earth shall be blessed in his seed (Gen. xii:3, xviii:18, xxii:18). The same promise was given to Isaac (Gen. xxvi:4) and to Jacob (Gen. xxviii:14). The promise to Isaac was connected with a manifestation of the Lord, a Theophany. The same took place in Jacob's life, when the Lord appeared unto him when he fled from Esau and was on the way to Haran.

No other Messianic promise is found in Genesis till we come to the dying bed of Jacob. We do not relate here the remarkable story of one of the sons of the aged patriarch, Joseph. The experience of this much beloved son of Jacob reveals a most startling providence and at the same time it is one of the clearest and fascinating forecasts of the suffering and glory of the promised seed.

When the hour of departure had come aged Jacob called his twelve sons to gather around his couch. While his eyes were soon to close on earthly things another vision is given to him, he speaks of the future and becomes a prophet. Through which of his sons is the promise of the seed to be perpetuated? Reuben stands first, followed by Simeon and Levi. All three had forfeited the right of primogeniture. Reuben had committed incest; the other two had done that frightful deed against the people of Shechem. When Jacob names Judah next he burst forth in a great prophecy.

"Judah, thee thy brethren shall praise! Thy hand shall be in the necks of thine enemies, thy father's children shall bow down to thee. Judah is a lion's whelp, from the prey, my son, thou art gone up. He stooped down, he shall lie down as a lion; and as a lioness. Who dares to arouse him? The sceptre shall not depart from Judah, nor a lawgiver from between his feet, until *Shiloh* come; and to Him shall the obedience of the peoples be. Binding his foal to the vine, and his ass's colt to the choice vine, he hath washed his clothing in wine, and his garment in the blood of grapes. His eyes shall be red with wine, and his teeth are white with milk" (Gen. ixl:8-12).

The question is, who is the Shiloh, to whom the peoples will yield obedience? First of all it is evident that the tribe of Judah is set apart as the royal tribe, the lion tribe. We are here reminded of two passages in the New Testament, which must be linked with the words of Jacob. The Lord Jesus Christ, the promised seed, we read of Him in Hebrews vii:14; "For it is evident that our Lord sprang from Judah." Then Jacob mentioned in connection with Judah the lion. Every Christian knows that in Revelation our Lord, in whom the promise of the seed is fulfilled, is called, "the Lion of the tribe of Judah" (Rev. v:5). This is conclusive evidence that Jacob announced prophetically that the seed should come from the tribe of Judah.

A regular philological and theological battle has raged around the word *Shiloh*. Criticism disputes the fact that it is the name of the person of the Messiah, in spite of the fact that ancient Jewish sources paraphrased the word by saying, "This is King Messiah."* Some state, like Delitzsch, and others that it is a place. Some say that it means "One sent"; others again amended the text and claim it means "the desired one." Other suggestions are the following, "until that comes which belongs to him" (to Judah) and "until he comes to whom it (the sceptre) belongs." Astonishing is the following assertion, "We have furthermore the fact that no such name as *Shiloh* is given to the Messiah elsewhere in the Old Testament. In the development of the Messianic idea, such a name has no subsequent unfolding." We differ from these scholars. The root from which the word is derived is *Sholoh*. It means "quiet, restful, peaceful". From it spring the different words express-

---

*Talmud: Tract Sanhedrin.

ing peace.   Shiloh means "Man of Peace"; for the first time
we have the hint, that the seed of the woman, from Shem, the
seed of Abraham, coming from the tribe of Judah will be,
"Peace."   But even if Shiloh were not one of Messiah's name
the fact remains that the inspired dying Jacob predicted that
the seed should come out of the tribe of Judah.

Before we come to the family, or house, from which the
promised seed was to come, we must mention several other
Messianic prophecies recorded in the Pentateuch.   The first
came from the lips of the heathen sorcerer Balaam.   It
was at the close of the forty years of Israel's wanderings.
A dreadful fear had taken hold on Balak, king of Moab, on
account of the victorious Israelites.   He turned in his despair
to Balaam to induce him to cast a spell upon the advancing
hosts of Israel and to curse them.   Like Judas and Simon
Magus in the New Testament, Balaam is ready to do it for
the love of money.   He must have had a wide reputation
that his powers to bless and to curse were effective.   And now
that voice speaks outside the fold of Israel.   When he opens
his lips he is forced to bless instead of the cursing the king of
Moab had demanded.   His parables are prophetic.   Balaam
speaks of Israel's blessing, Israel's glory and Israel's future.
Then he had a great vision.   He saw a *star* rising out of
Jacob and a *sceptre* out of Israel (Num. xxiv:17-19).
That sceptre is to smite Moab and subdue all nations and
destroy all enemies.   Both star and sceptre reveal the seed
of the woman, the seed of Abraham of the tribe of Judah.
Thus the hope is personified, for star and sceptre denote a
person.   The wise men came (Matt. ii) with the message,
"We have seen His star."   Our Lord applies the word "star"
to Himself as well as the sceptre (Rev. ii:27; xxii:16).   When
in the second century of our era, during the reign of Hadrian,
a false Christ appeared amongst the Jews, he called himself
Bar Cochva—"Son of the Star."

Another prediction is found in the eighteenth chapter of
Deuteronomy.   "I will raise them up a prophet from among
their brethren, like unto thee, and will put my words in his
mouth; and he shall speak unto them all that I shall com-

mand him. And it shall come to pass, that whosoever will
not hearken unto my words which he shall speak in my Name,
I will require it of him (Deut xviii:18, 19). We do not need
to follow the critical school with its denials as to this prediction. The New Testament gives the fullest sanction to
its Messianic interpretation. See (John i:21; vi:14; vii:40;
Acts iii:22-24; vii:37.)

But the prophecy as to the seed of the woman, the seed to
spring from Abraham of the race of Shem, from the tribe of
Judah is finally narrowed down to one house, one family,
of that tribe. We turn for a starting point to an impressive
scene recorded in the Second Book of Samuel (2 Sam. vii).
The great warrior king David had reached a time of peace.
The Lord had subdued all his enemies and had given him
rest. We see him seated in his house and Nathan the prophet is with him. No longer is the king's mind occupied
with the problems of war. Something else is on his heart.
He turned to the prophet of God and said, "See now I dwell
in a house of cedar, but the ark of God dwelleth within
curtains." The desire in his heart was to build a house for
Jehovah in his capital Jerusalem. Nathan probably knew
of all the materials which had been gathered for the erection
of a temple. He answered the king, "Go do all that is in
thine heart; for the Lord is with thee." He meant well, but
he spoke not as a prophet. It was not the Lord's message
but his own. That same night the Lord spoke to Nathan to
bring to David another message. Not David is to build a
house for the Lord, but the Lord will build him a house.
We find the record also in 1 Chronicles xvii:10-14.

"Furthermore I tell thee that the Lord will build thee an house.
And it shall come to pass, when thy days be expired that thou must
go to be with thy fathers, that I will raise up thy seed after thee, which
shall be of thy sons; and I will establish thy kingdom. He shall build
me an house, and I will establish his throne forever. I will be his
father, and he shall be my son; and I will not take my mercy away
from him, as I took it from him that was before thee. But I will
settle him in mine house and in my kingdom for ever, and his throne
shall be established forevermore."

In the other passage we find additional words: "If he

commit iniquity, I will chasten him with the rods of men, and with the stripes of the children of men" (2 Sam. vii:14). In this, suffering is announced on account of iniquity. Most commentators apply these words of Nathan to Solomon, the illustrious son of David. But Solomon is only a type of another one, who in His holy humanity is the son of David, the promised seed. Not Solomon but David's Lord and David's son (Psa. cx:1) has an everlasting throne. We should note that the seed in the above quoted passage is to be raised up after David had been gathered to be with his fathers. But Solomon was in his early manhood when his father died. So logically it must mean a future son of David, whose kingdom shall be established, who will build an house and whose throne shall be established for ever. As to committing iniquity and the chastisement on account of it cannot be applied to Him, who later is called the Holy One of Israel. Yet in another sense through His vicarious suffering, redemption and glory is procured. As we shall find elsewhere the seed suffers not for His own sins, which He had not, but for the sins of others.

But let us also listen to the last words of David as they are recorded in 2 Samuel xxiii:1-5:

"The Spirit of Jehovah speaks in me, and His Word is upon my tongue. The God of Israel said, the rock of Israel speaks to me. A ruler over men, righteous, a ruler in the fear of God. He shall be as the morning light when the sun riseth, a morning without clouds, after shining and rain, tender grass springs from the earth. Is not thus my house with God? For He hath made with me an everlasting covenant, arranged in all things and sure. For this is all my salvation, and all my desire. Will He not make it to grow?'' (Correct translation.)

The two verses which follow in David's last words speak of the judgment of the righteous ruler, how He will deal with His adversaries. The righteous ruler, who comes "as the morning light when the sun rises," who brings "a morning without clouds," who will judge and rule, is not Solomon, but the promised seed, the Messiah.

All doubt as to the meaning of the Davidic covenant, the

promised seed, who shall have the throne and a perpetual kingdom, is removed by the predictions which follow in the Psalms and in the prophetic books. We reserve the Messianic testimony of the Psalms, David's prophetic utterances as to the suffering and glory, the heel and head crushing, for a future chapter. Here we call attention to a few texts from different Bible books.

"And there shall come forth a rod out of the stem of Jesse (David's father), and a Branch shall grow out of his roots; and the Spirit of the Lord shall rest upon him; the spirit of wisdom and understanding; the spirit of counsel and might; the spirit of knowledge, and of the fear of the Lord" (Isa. xi:1-2).

This prophecy and the entire chapter reveals the promised seed, David's seed, and the work which that seed will accomplish.

We link with this passage a confirming prophecy of Jeremiah:

"Behold the days come, saith the Lord, that I will raise unto David a righteous Branch, and a King shall reign and prosper and shall execute judgment and justice in the earth. In his days Judah shall be saved and Israel shall dwell safely; and this is the name whereby he shall be called, the Lord our righteousness" (Jer. xxiii:5-6).

No such king ever reigned, nor is today David's throne filled by one who reigns and rules in righteousness and under whom Judah and Israel enjoy perfect safety. That King is the Hope of Israel and the Hope of the world. Still more assuring are Jeremiah's words in another chapter.

"And the Word of the Lord came unto Jeremiah, saying, Thus saith the Lord. If ye can break my covenant of the day and my covenant of the night, that there should not be day and night in their season; then may also my covenant with David be broken, my servant, that he should not have a son to reign upon his throne" (xxxiii:20-21).

We must next mention a few prophecies which unfold the seed of the woman, the seed of Abraham and the seed of David, as to His coming, and His Person.

We quote first a prophecy which is addressed, under peculiar circumstances, to the house of David. Ahaz, the son of Jotham, was king of Judah. He was threatened by a powerful alliance. Rezin, the king of Syria, and Pekah, the king of Israel, were marching on Jerusalem. The cowardly king of Judah trembled and the nation with him. The Prophet Isaiah had received a message for the king which he communicated unto him. "Take heed, and be quiet; fear not, neither be faint-hearted" (Isa. vii:4). Concerning the plottings of the enemy, the Lord sent him another message, "It shall not stand, neither shall it come to pass." It seems there was no answer from Ahaz. So finally Jehovah spoke again: "Ask thee a sign from Jehovah thy God; ask it either in the depth, or in the height above." Yet Ahaz refused under the plea that he would not tempt the Lord. Then the Lord answered the king of Judah.

"And he said, Hear ye now, O house of David, Is it a small thing for you to weary me, but will ye weary my God also? Therefore the Lord Himself will give you a sign: Behold the virgin shall conceive, and bear a son, and shall call His name Immanuel" (Isa. vii:13, 14).

We do not enter into the supposed difficulties of this passage. It is not the purpose of this volume to cite the objections made by the school of destructive criticism and to answer them. Today the modernistic schools, colleges, and seminaries, in spite of the definite assurance given in the first chapter of the New Testament that the virgin-born son, whose name is "God with us," is the Messiah, the promised seed, Modernism rejects both the prophecy of Isaiah and the divinely inspired comment in Matthew i:22-23. We let another speak who was himself a critic, yet not destructive but constructive.

"This pledge (the virgin-birth of Immanuel) was given in a period of impending distress. It remained a predicted pledge until the birth of the Messiah. There is no reason why we should seek a fulfilment of the sign in the time of Ahaz. It is a sign which was expressly assigned to the future. It matters little whether the prophet or his hearers looked for a speedy fulfilment. It was not for them to measure the times and intervals of the divine plan of redemption. If they looked for the birth of such a son in the time of Ahaz or Hezekiah, they were disappointed. There is no historical evidence of any such birth or of any such child. The names assigned to the children of the prophet (Isaiah) are plain enough, but there is no connection of

this name with any of his children. If, however, any one should prefer
to think that a child of the prophet or the royal house bore this name
as a sign, the prediction then would become typical and cease to be
direct prediction, but the Messianic idea would not be lost. This
Immanuel would then be a type of the great Immanuel, just as David
and Moses and Solomon and others have been such types of the
Messiah. The passage is a Messianic passage, and the prelude to the
predictions of the Messianic king which follow in Isaiah and in Micah.
Isaiah subsequently gives the child to be born many sacred names and
Micah points to the birthplace in Bethlehem."*

There is no liberalist today who endorses these scholarly
remarks, nor would they be accepted in any theological
school in which modern rationalism is taught.

We learn then from this great fundamental passage that
the seed of the woman springs from *the* virgin,† and that the
virgin is of the house of David. The name of the seed,
"Immanuel"—God with us—is the first great announcement
in Scripture that the seed will be supernatural. This is
more fully revealed in another prophetic utterance of Isaiah.

"For unto us a child is born, unto us a son is given; and the government shall be upon his shoulder, and his name shall be called, Wonderful, Counsellor, The mighty God, The everlasting Father, The
Prince of Peace. Of the increase of his government and peace there
shall be no end, upon the throne of David, and upon his kingdom to
order it, and to establish it with judgment and with justice from henceforth even for ever. The zeal of the Lord of hosts will perform this"
(Isa. ix:6-7).

The prophet is projected into the future and beholds the
event as already accomplished. This answers the objection
which has been raised that the words must be applied to a
child born in the days of Isaiah. In the first sentence, "For
unto us a child is born", the virgin born one is seen. But
He is more than a human being, "*A son is given.*" The
names of Deity follow. The son given, a gift, is the Only
Begotten of the Father. This God-man, the Immanuel, on
the human side of the house of David, receives the government, the throne of David and the kingdom.

---

*Charles A. Briggs, "Messianic Prophecy."

†The Hebrew has the definite article.

It is written, "The testimony of Jesus is the spirit of prophecy" (Rev. xix:10). The Greek *Jesus* is the same as the Hebrew *Joshua—Jehovah saves*. We find therefore as we listen to the voice of the prophets of God that they announced the coming One increasingly as Jehovah manifested in the flesh. *Jehovah Himself is the great Hope.* Isaiah saw Him and His glory in his vision (Isa. vi:1-4; John xii:41). Many times the great prophet pens His name in his God-breathed messages as "the Holy One of Israel." This Holy One is both Creator and Redeemer. He speaks as the Creator of heaven and earth (Isa. xlv:12). The same is the Redeemer. "For I am Jehovah thy God, the Holy One of Israel, thy Saviour" (Isa. xliii:3).

"Thus saith Jehovah, your Redeemer, the Holy One of Israel" (Isa. xliii:14). "Thus saith Jehovah, thy Redeemer, the Holy One of Israel" (Isa. xlviii:17). "I Jehovah am thy Saviour and thy Redeemer, the mighty One of Jacob" (Isa. xlix:26). He speaks of Himself as "the first and the last" (Isa. xliv:6). We listen to Him again and He declares He is "a just God and a Saviour" and calls "Look unto Me, and be ye saved all the ends of the earth" (Isa. xlv:21, 22). Isaiah also describes this Holy One as Jehovah the Servant, who comes to serve and to suffer and is rejected by Israel. They despise and abhor Him (Isa. xlix:7). Our next chapter will follow the suffering of the seed as revealed in the Word of God.

Micah the Morasthite was the contemporary of Isaiah. He announced prophetically the birthplace of the promised seed. "But thou, Bethlehem Ephrata, though thou be little among the thousands of Judah, yet out of thee shall He come forth unto me that is to be ruler in Israel; whose goings forth have been from of old, from everlasting" (Micah v:2). The last sentence of this prophecy shows again that the seed will be Jehovah, the Immanuel.

And so throughout the entire prophetic Word He who is the seed of the woman, the great Hope, is revealed as Jehovah.

CHAPTER III

Hope and Redemption Through His Suffering

Some nineteen hundred years ago on a bright and glorious day of spring two persons were walking along a country road. They had just left Jerusalem and were on their way to a small village, called Emmaus. One of them was Cleopas, the other may have been his wife, or some other disciple. They were engaged in an earnest conversation over a very perplexing matter. Their countenances showed worry and sadness. Suddenly another person appeared and joined their company. The stranger addressed them at once, "What manner of communications are these that ye have one to another, as ye walk, and are sad?" At this question they expressed surprise. Surmising that the stranger also came from Jerusalem, they said: "Art thou only a stranger in Jerusalem, and hast not known these things which are come to pass in these days?" It brought forth an inquiry from their new companion, "What things?"

Then both related to him the story of one, whom they called a prophet, mighty in deed and in word before God and all the people, Jesus of Nazareth. The chief priests and rulers had delivered him to be condemned to death and had crucified him. Freely they expressed their faith and hope in Him, trusting that He might have been Israel's promised Redeemer. His condemnation and crucifixion had happened just three days ago. And now on this third day, the first day of the week, the day after their Sabbath, strange reports had reached them. His body had been buried in a rock-hewn sepulchre. Certain women had gone early to the sepulchre. They found it empty. His body was not there. They had seen angels and these said that the crucified One is alive. Others too went to the sepulchre. They confirmed the startling news of the women. Himself they did not see.

Yet while the stranger spoke their eyes were holden that they should not recognize Him. The very person of whom they spake was walking and talking with them.

Then came His reply: "O fools, and slow of heart to believe all that the prophets have spoken. Ought not Christ to have suffered these things and to enter into His glory?"

But the stranger did more than that. "And beginning at Moses and all the prophets, He expounded to them in all the Scriptures the things concerning Himself." No wonder when later He revealed Himself and they recognized Him, when "He took the bread and blessed it," they said: "Did not our heart burn within us, while He talked with us by the way, and while He opened unto us the Scriptures?" (Luke xxiv:13-32).

This wonderful person, whom they called Jesus of Nazareth, who had been crucified and buried, who arose on the third day, is the promised seed, the seed of the woman, the son of Abraham of Shem, the son of David of the tribe of Judah. He is more than that. He is Immanuel, God manifested in the flesh. In Him all the prophecies relating to "the crushing of the heel," the suffering, with their deeper meaning of redemption, have found their literal fulfilment.

Some thirty-three years before the incident on the road to Emmaus, a virgin in Nazareth had a remarkable experience. She was a godly soul trusting in Jehovah and in His promises. She belonged to those who waited for the promised salvation. Her name was Mary. She was espoused to Joseph of the house of David. She also was of the house of David as proved by her genealogy in Luke iii:24-38. Knowing her Hebrew Scriptures she knew the great promise of the prophet Isaiah concerning the virgin and her son Immanuel. Suddenly there stood before her a heavenly visitor, the angel Gabriel, who addressed her as no other woman had ever been addressed before her nor after her. "Hail, thou art highly favored, the Lord is with thee, blessed art thou among women." No wonder the virgin was troubled on account of this remarkable salutation brought by Gabriel from the throne of God to her humble Galilean home. Then the heavenly messenger delivered his message: "Fear not Mary, for thou hast found favor with God. And, behold, thou shalt conceive in thy womb, and bring forth a son, and shall call his name Jesus (Jehovah is salvation).   He shall be great, and shall be called the Son of the Highest; and the Lord God shall give unto Him the throne of His father David, and He shall reign over the house of Jacob for ever; and of His kingdom there shall be no end." An innocent question came then from the virgin's lips: "How shall this be seeing I know not a man?"   This question brought forth an additional revelation, a revelation of the greatest importance.   "And the angel answered and said unto her, The Holy Spirit shall come upon thee, and the power of the Highest shall overshadow thee, therefore also that holy thing which shall be born of thee shall be called the Son of God" (Luke i:26-35).   It reveals the mode of the virgin birth.   The Holy Spirit, the Spirit of Life and of power produced in the virgin a human body.   The body of the Immanuel was therefore the direct creation of the Spirit of God.   Jehovah, the Son, left the bosom of God, His everlasting dwelling place, and identified Himself with that body.   Thus the child was born and the Son given.

But we must add to this the testimony of the opening chapter of the New Testament.   The genealogy in Matthew is the genealogy of Joseph, the supposed father of Jesus (Luke iii:23).   Then follows the record of the birth of Jesus Christ.

"Now the birth of Jesus Christ was on this wise.   When His mother Mary was espoused to Joseph, before they came together, she was found with child of the Holy Spirit.   Then Joseph her husband, being a just man, and not willing to make her a public example, was minded to put her away privily.   But while he thought on these things, behold the angel of the Lord appeared unto him in a dream, saying, Joseph thou son of David, fear not to take unto thee Mary thy wife, for that which is conceived in her is of the Holy Spirit.   And she shall bring forth a son, and thou shalt call His name Jesus, for He shall save His people from their sins.   Now all this was done, that it might be fulfilled which was spoken of the Lord by the prophet, saying, Behold, a virgin shall be with child, and shall bring forth a son, and they shall call His name Immanuel, which is being interpreted, God with us. Then, Joseph being raised from sleep did as the angel of the Lord had bidden him, and took unto him his wife; and knew her not till she brought forth her firstborn son; and she called His name Jesus" (Matt. i:19-25).

How perfectly all fits together! Isaiah's great prophecy was thus fulfilled. Isaiah wrote seven hundred and fifty years before Christ. He had announced the virgin born One, His true humanity and His Deity. "But when the fulness of time was come, God sent forth His Son, made of a woman, made under the law" (Gal. iv:1).

Silence enshrouds the greater part of the life of the seed of the woman, the Immanuel, save a single incident, which it pleased the Holy Spirit to make known, when the twelve year old boy revealed His Deity in the Temple of Jerusalem, yet proved His humanity and humiliation by returning to Nazareth, "increasing in wisdom and stature, and in favor with God and man" (Luke ii:46-52).

There is in existence a spurious document called *Evangelium Infantum*—the Gospel of the infancy.* It contains such ridiculous, superstitious stories that its fraudulent character is clearly established. For instance, it claims that many miracles were performed by people using the water in which Mary had washed her infant; leprosy and other diseases were cured. Another document, *Thomas's Gospel of the Infancy*, relates even more puerile and unbelievable incidents of the child-life of our Lord. The early Church rightly rejected these counterfeits and legendary accounts. Scholars of the Rationalistic school, known as Modernists, claim that our four Gospels have been embellished by later hands by adding the miraculous to a primitive account so as to put the halo of the supernatural around Him, whom they call the Nazarene. Historically this assertion is a mere invention. The documentary evidences that our four Gospel records are genuine and entirely trustworthy are conclusive. To this we add the fact that these spurious accounts of the infancy of Jesus were most positively refused by the Church Fathers.

We begin where the Gospels begin in relating the public ministry of our Lord. We go to the banks of Jordan. There

---

*Professor Henry Sike, of Cambridge University, first translated this Gospel and had it published in 1697. It dates back to the third century. It was received by the sect of the Gnostics.

we behold the last of the great Old Testament Prophets, John the son of Zechariah, known as John the Baptist.   He is the voice crying in the wilderness, as announced by Isaiah: "The voice of him that crieth in the wilderness, Prepare ye the way of the Lord, make straight in the desert a highway for our God" (Isa. xl:3).   He came in the power and spirit of Elijah and if the Jewish nation had accepted Christ, he would have been the Elijah, according to the words of our Lord (Matt. xi:14).   He appeared as the herald of the promised King, the son of David and proclaimed the nearness of the Messianic Kingdom, because he knew the promised One was in their midst.

John's great message was the message of repentance. The baptism he practiced was unto repentance: Jordan is the type of death. Those who followed the call to repentance submitted to baptism in Jordan, a confession that they were sinners and had deserved death.

Then the God-Man, Jesus, came to be baptized of John. John refused for he knew His holy, His sinless character, yet he granted His request after he heard His words. What followed is of great meaning. Why did He submit to baptism? Why did He go into that river to express by His act that the sentence of death should also rest upon Him? The wages of sin is death. But He had no sin. How then could death be His portion?

He demanded the baptism in Jordan because He was fully conscious of the great work He had come to accomplish. That great work which would bring within the reach of all humanity the *Hope of Life and Glory*, was known to Him before the foundation of the world. All God's purposes center in this work. As mentioned before, when He announced in Eden the program and history of redemption, He knew what it would be. He would become in God's appointed time the seed of the woman, His heel would be crushed and He would utltimately crush the serpent's head. He knew redemption and victory necessitated suffering. The Hope of redemption and redemption itself could only come through Him and His suffering. The sentence of death could only be met by death. The penalty had to be paid. Reconciliation had to be effected; peace had to be made. The curse of sin had to be removed. Death and the grave had to be defeated.

When He stepped down to the brink of the river and John baptized Him, when the waters of Jordan covered Him and passed over His head, He showed that He had come to take the sinner's place in death. He indicated symbolically that He had come to take upon Himself the sufferings, so minutely foretold in the Scriptures of the Old Testament. According to the Gospel of John, written by the beloved disciple, John the Baptist pointed Him out to his own followers as the promised One, the Lamb of God, so abundantly foreshadowed in the God given Levitical worship, in the sacrifices and offerings of animals, and the approach to God through the shedding of their blood. When those Jews heard from John's lips the message, "Behold the Lamb of God," and again, "Behold the Lamb of God which taketh away the sin of the world" (John i:29, 36), they must have been at once reminded of types and prophecies; they must also have remembered the Passover experience of their fathers in Egypt and how the blood of the Passover lamb had wrought their redemption.

We cannot follow here the blessed footsteps of Him of whom John wrote, "And the Word was made flesh, and dwelt among us, and we beheld His glory, the glory as of the only begotten of the Father, full of grace and truth" (John i:14). His holy life, His meek and lowly character, His moral glory, all was the literal fulfilment of the Holy Spirit's predictions in the old Testament. We do not make a closer examination of the credentials of His Deity which He so wonderfully displayed during His three years ministry among His own. He came as the minister of the circumcision to confirm the promises made unto the fathers (Rom. xv:8). His credentials were the attributes of Godhead manifested in His miraculous acts. He manifested omnipotence by healing instantaneously, leprosy, palsy, fevers, all kinds of other diseases, besides restoring the maimed, the cripples who sought His

merciful help.   He healed by touch; He healed by His Word,
being absent from the sufferers.   He healed the blind, the
deaf and the dumb.   He had power over demons and over
all unclean spirits.   He had power over death, for He raised
the physically dead; and He had power over the forces of
nature.   He commanded the wind and the waves; He turned
water into wine; He multiplied five loaves and two fishes that
thousands were fed and much more left over.

He manifested Omniscience.   He knew the future and predicted what should take place; He knew the thoughts of His
disciples and all the plottings of His enemies were known to
Him.   Liberal Christendom, rationalistic modernism, which
denies the supernatural, claims that the miracles of Christ as
recorded in the four Gospel records are nothing but interpo-
lations, invented by certain men living many years after the
eye-witnesses were no longer here.   But take out from the
Gospel records the miraculous, and what is left?   Nothing
but an empty shell.   But such is the aim of infidelity, whether
baptized or unbaptized, to rob man in his sinful and miserable
existence of the hope and comfort, which are offered in the
God-Man, Jesus Christ.

We do not enlarge upon all this, but we turn to some of the
predicted sufferings of the Virgin-born Son of God, announced, as we have seen for the first time in Eden when man
sinned and became an alienated creature.

With many other readers and students of the Gospel of
Luke we have wished to know what Scriptures He used in
that memorable walk from Jerusalem to Emmaus on the day
of His resurrection, when He revealed unto them the Scriptures about His sufferings.   He began with Moses and all the
prophets.   We wonder if He began with Genesis iii:15 and
followed the explanation of His sacrificial work on the cross
by the types as recorded by Moses.   Later when Cleopas and
his companion had returned to Jerusalem to relate to the
gathered eleven disciples their Emmaus experience, He appeared again, after demonstrating that He was not a phan-
tom.   He appeared unto them in the same body He had given
on Calvary's Cross, showing unto them His hands and His

feet. And then He gave another Scripture exposition. "And He said unto them, These are the words I spake unto you, while I was yet with you, that all things must be fulfilled, which were written in the law of Moses, and in the Prophets, and in the Psalms concerning Me. Then opened He their understanding, that they might understand the Scriptures, and said unto them, Thus it is written, and thus it behooved Christ to suffer, and to rise from the dead the third day" (Luke xxiv:44-46).

During the days of His ministry He had made the challenge to, "search the Scriptures," and He added "they are they that testify of Me" (John v:39). Peter's pen, guided by the Holy Spirit, states that the prophets through the Spirit of Christ testified beforehand the sufferings of Christ, and the glory that should follow (1 Peter i:10-11). His disciples had heard from His lips several times, after the kingdom message addressed to Israel had been rejected, that they would deliver Him into the hands of the Gentiles, that He must suffer many things of the elders and chief priests and scribes, that He would be crucified, and be raised again the third day. They did not understand Him then; Peter even rebuked Him. But now He opened their understanding, as He still opens hearts and minds of those who believe the same Scriptures, by the Paraclete, the Holy Spirit.

We notice that the Psalms are mentioned by Him. They are found in the Hebrew Bible in the portion called the *Kethubim*, the writings. He had quoted frequently the Psalms in His earthly ministry, but now He used them to show how the sufferings of Himself were all pre-written in the Psalms, and that He had fulfilled them. Though no information is given what Psalms He used we can take it for granted that He must have used the twenty-second Psalm, because in this Psalm is given one of the completest prophecies concerning the sufferings of Himself. In all probability He referred to this remarkable prophecy when He showed unto them His hands and His feet, in which the prints of the nails were seen.

So we turn briefly to this great Psalm, given by the Spirit

of God, to David.   No true believer in God's Word doubts
this fact, for the inscription says "A Psalm of David."   Yet
one of the most recommended works on the Psalms states,
"It is more probable that this Psalm was composed by one of
the exiles during the Babylonian captivity".*   Other critics
like Baur and Ewald deny the Davidic authorship, and say
it was composed hundreds of years later.   Some, like Olshausen, declare that the Psalm must have been written during
the days of the Maccabees.   Besides the inscription everything in this Psalm, in comparison with other Davidic Psalms,
bears witness that David wrote it.   The orthodox synagogue
has always credited the Psalm to David.   He must have
written it during one of the severe persecutions he suffered,
persecutions which are prophetically typical of the sufferings
of Christ.   Yet the deep agony and terrible suffering described in it were *never* David's.   He did not pass through
any such experience.   Nor can the glory, which follows the
suffering in this Psalm, be applied to David.   Before his
vision passed something which was not his own experience,
and historically we cannot locate anything in King David's
life which would answer to this prophecy.   Perhaps after he
wrote down these terrible sufferings, he read and read again
his own words, without grasping fully their meaning.   He described one who suffered, though he trusted God.   It was the
Holy Spirit who "testified of the sufferings of Christ," who is
according to the flesh, the son of David.   Needless to say that
the New Testament applies this Psalm to Christ and His
great work on the cross.

The great prophecy in its scope is extremely simple.
Suffering stands first (verses 1-21); Glory follows, (verses
22-31).   Two Hebrew words are found in the inscription—
"*Aijeleth Shahar*"—"the hind of the morning."   Some have
applied these words to Christ's suffering and resurrection.
They say, "the wounded hind suffers innocently, but the
dawn of the morning brings relief."   Jewish tradition gives
a better meaning.   They say *Aijeleth Shahar* refers to the

*Stewart Perowne, "The Book of Psalms."

Schekina, the glory cloud which was visibly present in the midst of Israel. The dawning of the morning is compared by them to the horns of a hind, because the rays of light appear like the horns of that animal. They speak of the two words as meaning, "the dawning of redemption." According to their tradition the morning sacrifice, a lamb, was offered as soon as the watchers on the pinnacle of the temple beheld the first rays of the morning. Then they cried out, "Behold the first rays of the morning shine forth." Thus the blessed dawning of redemption through Christ the Lamb of God is revealed in this Psalm.

But what pen can describe the sufferings of the Holy One, sufferings which our poor finite minds can never fathom!

The twenty-second Psalm begins with that deep cry of agony, the cry of mystery. "My God, My God why hast Thou forsaken Me?" He who is Immanuel, the seed of the woman, yet God manifested in the flesh, was forsaken of God, in the sufferings of the cross. He whose meat and drink was to do the Father's will, who glorified God in His holy spotless, sinless life, the Virgin-born Son of God, forsaken of God! It is the mystery of all mysteries. *Eli, Eli, lama sabachthani?* were uttered by His lips as darkness, greater than the Egyptian darkness, enshrouded the cross. We are face to face with the unsearchable depths of His work as the sin-bearer. He who in His life on earth was always in fellowship with God, was forsaken of God. It was then that He bore the curse of sin and the wrath of the righteous God. It was then that He, who knew no sin was made sin for us. Forsaken of God! Heaven's darkness bore witness to it. Heaven had no answer to His cry; no angel came to strengthen Him. The penalty of sin, the full penalty, which in its enormity we cannot understand, had to be paid. In the language of God's own Word, "All the waves and billows broke over His head" and "He was laid into the lowest pit." What must have been His agony as He was forsaken of God! What suffering when the sword smote the fellow of God! (Zech. xiii:10). Yet while there is no answer from heaven to the question, He Himself out of the densest darkness answers that question. "Why hast Thou forsaken Me?" His answer justifies God. "But Thou art holy" (Verse 4). The holiness of God is the solution of this cry of mystery. What did it all mean? He stood as the sin-bearer in the presence of the God of Holiness, the God of Light "in Whom there is no darkness at all" (1 John i:5). Then the great transaction, involving our redemption was done.

And how significant it is that just this cry of deepest suffering is put into the foreground of this Psalm! Had man written of this sufferer, he would have given first of all an elaborate description of the physical sufferings, what man did to torment the holy victim. Man would have put *first* the horrible and sickening details of crucifixion. But the Holy Spirit puts the physical sufferings of the God-Man into the background, and puts first the cry of the forsaken One. Why? We give the answer of another. "No act of man could make Him sin for man—no suffering from men could make atonement with God; that was wrought by what passed between God and His burdened soul within that curtained chamber, never to be penetrated by any foot but His, and from which no cry emerges but that pregnant one, the meaning of which is here revealed as far as may be for the satisfaction of our conscience and the adoring worship of our hearts. What man wrought could only naturally bring judgment upon man. What He wrought with God, and through Him, brings out from the smitten Rock the river of divine omnipotent grace." On the threshold of this great Psalm we find the atoning work of the seed of the woman, God manifested in the flesh, in its deep Godward aspect, the only source of grace, unfathomable grace, for guilty, lost sinners. He, Immanuel is the great, yes, the only hope of redemption which man has and ever will have.

We know from our Gospels that, when at last the darkness was gone, He uttered, not the cry of defeat, but the shout of victory, "It is finished!" Here is another blessed fact. The Psalm begins with the cry of the forsaken One, it ends with a word which fully corresponds to the "It is finished!", of the cross. *He hath done it* (Psa. xxii:31). We ask What?

The glory side of this Psalm gives an answer.   Yes, all that is
in store in blessing for this earth and all the glories of eternity
are the results of the work of the cross, the sufferings of the
promised seed.

And now follow other prophecies of deep interest written
a thousand years before their literal fulfillment in the Christ
of God, the man of sorrows and acquainted with grief.   In
reading these remarkable predictions one is reminded of
Jeremiah's lament, "Is it nothing to you, all ye that pass by?
Behold and see if there be any sorrow like unto my sorrow
which is brought upon me, wherewith Jehovah has afflicted
me in the day of His fierce anger" (Lam. i:12).

In the second verse "the night season" mentioned may
be applied to Gethsemane.   "But I am a worm and not a
man, a reproach of men and despised of the people" (Verse 6).
These are His own words.   The Hebrew word "worm" is the
word used for a small insect, the *coccus*, which in its death
yields a scarlet color.   It is the very color obtained by the
Israelites for the use in the tabernacle.   Thus He died that
our sins, though red as scarlet, might be white as snow.

Next we find in this prophetic Psalm foretold the reproach
and the mockeries of the people.   Men reproached Him; His
own rejected and despised Him.   "They laugh Me to scorn";
—"They shoot out the lip";—"They shake the head."   Then
we read the taunt, "He trusted in the Lord that He should
deliver Him, seeing He delighted in Him" (Verse 8).   And in
all He trusted in God.   Yea, from His mother's, the Virgin's
womb, He trusted God.   What a glimpse it gives of Him who
is, "The Wonderful."   Only He and no other one could
speak thus!

Here we find a description of His enemies, the dogs and the
assembly of the wicked, Gentiles and Jews.   Satan is seen as
"the ravening and roaring lion."   Then follows a detailed
description of crucifixion.   This mode of death was unknown
among the ancient Hebrews.   It was invented by cruel,
pagan Rome.   Yet this Psalm gives a complete picture of
this horrible form of death.   "I am poured out like water"
—excessive perspiration.   "All my bones are out of joint"—

disjointed arms, shoulders and limbs. "My heart is like wax"—an affected heart. "My strength is dried up"—extreme weakness. "My tongue cleaveth to my jaws,"—terrible thirst. "I can count all my bones"—every bone affected. "Hands and feet pierced." Then we read, "They look and stare upon me," they gloat over His sufferings. His garments are taken from Him; they are parted amongst the soldiers and they gamble for His vesture (Verse 18). But while the sufferer speaks of what men did unto Him, it is also revealed that neither man nor Satan could touch His life and put Him to death. He addresses God, "Thou hast brought Me into the dust of death." The death He suffered was according to the will of God and therefore an act of Obedience, "He was obedient unto death, the death of the cross."

How he must have spoken to them of this great Psalm and how all was fulfilled as He hung on that cross. Every detail had been accomplished.

But His sufferings are also written in scores of other Psalms. There are but few in the entire collection of Psalms which mention suffering and which do not refer to His own sufferings. We call attention to the fortieth Psalm, the sixty-ninth and the one hundred and ninth. How well He knew what was written in all of them concerning Himself. He knew the brief prophecy in Psalm lxix:21. And that "the Scripture might be fulfilled, He said, I thirst" (John xix:28, 29). One prediction after another as written in the Psalms came to pass, not one remained unfulfilled, till finally He bowed His thorn-crowned head, after His victorious shout announcing His finished work, and there He used another word given in a Psalm, saying "Father, into Thy hands I commend My Spirit" (Psa. xxxi:5).

Perhaps He also reminded His disciples of that greatest of all prophecies, concerning His substitutionary sacrifice, the fifty-third chapter in Isaiah. The servant Jehovah rejected by His own is seen in this wonderful prediction as the sin-bearer. As it is well known apostate Christendom has fallen in line with apostate Judaism, generally called and known by the name of "Reformed Judaism," which claims that the suffering servant, so vividly portrayed by Isaiah, is not an individual, but the Jewish nation. We let another speak, who was known as a higher critic, yet did not reject the Messianic prophecy of this chapter.

"He is pierced and scourged, and crushed, and suffers cruel persecution. But this is not the cause of His agony. He suffers for sin, and that not His own. He is an innocent sufferer, whose grief is enhanced by injustice and wrong, and is intensified by the keen apprehension of the ill-desert of those for whom He suffers. All else have strayed from the fold of God, He only is faithful, and Jehovah imposes upon Him, the sum of the iniquity of the people. As the only faithful and innocent One, He comes to the front, stands in the breach and takes upon Himself the curse of the nation. We cannot see in this sin-bearing servant any other than *an individual*, for the author of the prophecy includes himself with all others, whose sins the servant bears, and for whose redemption He suffers. . . . "

"The Prophet finally represents that this suffering has been in order to accomplish a divine plan of redemption. He suffers in obedience to the divine appointment. He offers a trespass-offering for the sins of the people, in order to purchase their redemption. His death is such a substitution and compensation for sin. When this has been accomplished, the condition of humiliation has come to an end, and the exaltation of the servant begins. There is no explicit mention of resurrection, but this is implicitly involved. The rewards are success in His ministry, the enjoyment of the spoils of His victory, and exaltation to great honor as the Redeemer. This prophecy of the servant who dies and rises from the grave, finds *its only fulfilment in the death of Jesus Christ, and in His resurrection and exaltation to the heavenly throne.*"*

*These extracts are from "Messianic Prophecy," by Charles A. Briggs, D.D., New York. Charles Scribner's Sons, 1886. Dr. Briggs belonged to the school of "Higher Criticism," and was professor in Union Theological Seminary in New York City. We quote from this work again to show the advance of the critical school becoming the

But how much there is written in prophecy concerning the sufferings of Christ, the promised seed! Nor is it in direct prophecy alone, we find the same truth in types and in history. It is not the purpose of this volume to develop these facts of prophecy relating to the sufferings of Christ.

All the predicted sufferings as revealed in the Old Testament, in Moses, the Prophets and the Psalms, have found their literal fulfilment in Him, whom they called "Jesus of Nazareth," the son of David, born of the Virgin. He came to bring salvation to lost humanity. The purpose of His coming is stated in one sentence, "He came to put away sin by the sacrifice of Himself" (Heb. ix:26). This He did by His death on the cross. Only through Him can man, guilty and lost, have peace with God. "The Just One died for the unjust that He might bring us to God" 1 Peter iii:18). No man can come to the Father but by Him (John xiv:6). What that salvation is and includes for all believing individuals the Holy Spirit has fully and blessedly revealed in the great doctrinal epistles of the New Testament. We must look at it briefly. We must show how He, the seed of the woman, the Virgin-born Son of God, the Immanuel, is the great hope for lost humanity, that His finished work on the Cross meets all the need man has as a sinner.   Let us look briefly at these needs and how graciously and fully they are supplied in the blessed work of the great sin-bearer, the seed of the woman, our Lord Jesus Christ.

What then are man's spiritual needs? Through the first man, Adam, humanity has received a fallen nature, the sin-nature. This is denied in the camp of Modernism, yet evolution, that anti-christian hypothesis, gives no explanation of the existent evil, nor holds out any hope whatever of any improvement nor promises deliverance from the octopus which holds the race in its deadly grasp, which the Bible calls sin. The sin-nature produces its fruits in sins. The lust of the flesh, the lust of eyes, and the pride of life produce an

school of destructive criticism. It illustrates the progress of the apostasy. No outspoken Modernist allows today that the suffering servant portrayed in the fifty-third chapter of Isaiah is Christ.

existence which is enmity against God. Man is therefore an enemy of God. Well did one say in the Old Testament, "Mine iniquities are more than the hairs of mine head" (Psa. xl:12).

Man has no peace and knows no rest. In his breast is an accusing conscience. Upon him rests the heavy load of guilt. He is in a state of alienation from His Maker. He needs reconciliation to God, and also the definite and positive assurance that he is acquitted from the sentence of condemnation which the holy and righteous God has pronounced upon Him. He needs to know that the guilt of his sins is no more, that it has been removed, and that he is righteously acquitted. He needs the assurance that God has accepted him that there is now a settled peace with God. He needs the assurance that God is His Father and that he is a child of God. He needs the assuring hope as to an eternity of peace and glory. He needs a new nature, a nature divinely given, from which springs a new life of righteousness and holiness. Inasmuch as man is dead in trespasses and sins, helpless to do anything for himself, utterly without strength; if these needs are to be fully met and supplied, God must do it for man. If man is absolutely impotent to save himself, then God must save him. He has done so in His Son. His sacrificial work on the cross is what has accomplished for human beings who believe on Him, and accept Him, all we have stated and infinitely more. The Son of God, the seed of the woman, our Lord Jesus Christ therefore is the only hope. Apart from Him there is no hope in time and in eternity. As our own words are insufficient to make this known, we let the Word of God speak.

"For God so loved the world that He gave His Only Begotten Son, that whosoever believeth on Him, should not perish but have everlasting life" (John iii:16).

"Who His own self bare our sins in His own body on the tree" (1 Peter ii:24).

"For all have sinned, and come short of the glory of God; being justified freely by His grace through the redemption that is in Christ Jesus, whom God hath set forth a propitiation (mercy-seat) through faith in His blood, to declare His righteousness for the remission of sins that are past through the forbearance of God(*); to declare at this time His righteousness, that He might be just and the justifier of him that believeth in Jesus" (Rom. iii:23:26). "Christ died for our sins" (1 Cor. xv:3). "The Blood of Jesus Christ His Son cleanseth us from all sin" (1 John i:7).

"For if when we were enemies we were reconciled by the death of His Son, much more being reconciled, we shall be saved by His life" (His life as priest and advocate at the right hand of God) (Rom. v:10). "God was in Christ reconciling the world unto Himself, not imputing their trespasses unto them; and hath committed unto us the word of reconciliation. Now then we are ambassadors for Christ, as though God did beseech you by us; we pray you in Christ's stead, be ye reconciled unto God. For He hath made Him sin for us who knew no sin, that we might be made the righteousness of God in Him" (2 Cor. v:19-21). "In whom we have redemption through His Blood, the forgiveness of sins, according to the riches of His grace" (Ephes. i:7). "Being justified by faith we have peace with God through our Lord Jesus Christ" (Rom. v:1). "But now in Christ Jesus ye who sometimes were far off are made nigh by the Blood of Christ" (Ephes. ii:13). "Much more then, being justified by His Blood, we shall be saved from wrath through Him" (Rom. v:9). "He has washed us from our sins in His own Blood" (Rev. i:5). "Thou hast redeemed us unto God by Thy Blood" (Rev. v:9). "There is therefore now no condemnation to them which are in Christ Jesus" (Rom. viii:1). "What shall we then say to these things? If God be for us who can be against us? He that spared not His own Son, but delivered Him up for us all, how shall He not with Him also freely give us all things? Who shall lay anything to the charge of God's elect? It is God that justifieth" (Rom.

---

*The sins which are past are the sins of Old Testament Saints, who also believed in the promised seed and His work of redemption. They were justified in anticipation of Christ's death on the cross (see Rom. iv:1-12).

viii:31-33). And how many more pages could be filled with these precious words of life and glory!

This then is the first part of the hope of the ages, announced first by Himself and fully consummated by Him in giving His life on the Cross. From that cross sounds now forth God's good news, the Gospel of our salvation. Through Isaiah's pen He announced that news of redemption and hope should be heralded even unto the ends of the earth, "Look unto Me, and be ye saved all the ends of the earth, for I am God and there is none else" (Isa. xlv:22). And so it has been and so it is. The ends of the earth have heard and hear the message of hope and salvation through Him who is that hope. Heaven above has been filled with uncountable disembodied spirits, who absent from the body, are present with the Lord, yet are still consciously waiting and hoping what is promised unto them, "the redemption of the body." And on earth multitudes are trusting in Him as their only hope; they know that "the Gospel of Christ is the power of God unto salvation to the Jew first and also to the Greek." The proclamation of love and hope, the message of life and power, will continue till the revealed purpose of God during this present age is finished, till God the Holy Spirit has completed His work. What follows then? We shall find there is an unfulfilled hope which must be realized. The heel has been crushed; the serpent's head must also be crushed. Sufferings are past; but full glory is still future.

Once more we glance briefly at that scene when John had baptized Jesus in the river Jordan. We saw its typical meaning how He manifested in this act the mission for which He had come into the world, to take the sinner's place in death. But we also read, "The Heavens were opened unto Him" (Matt. iii:16). When our Lord left the waters, which typify death and the grave, we have a foreshadowing of resurrection; the heavens opening for Him signify His ascension into glory.

His resurrection is therefore the hope of all who trust in Him. Believers have "a living hope by the resurrection of Jesus Christ from among the dead, to an inheritance incorruptible, and undefiled, and that fadeth not away." It is reserved in heaven and all who have Him as their hope, "are kept by the power of God through faith unto salvation to be revealed in the last time" (1 Peter i:3-5). He conquered death and the grave. "O death where is thy sting; O grave where is thy victory"! (1 Cor. xv:55). He ascended into heaven, yea the Heaven of all heavens, and as the glorified Man took His seat at the right hand of God, "Angels and authorities and powers being made subject unto Him"(1 Peter iii:22). He has gone to heaven welcomed by the Father and proclaimed priest after the order of Melchisedek. He has gone to heaven to "Appear in the presence of God for us" (Heb. ix:24). He has gone to heaven to prepare a place for His own, who constitute His mystical body, His bride (John xiv:1-3). He has gone to heaven to carry on His present work, keeping by His intercession His own in the conflicts of the age; restoring them by His advocacy and in a larger sense upholding all things by the word of His power.

There faith sees Him, "crowned with glory and honor." There we behold Him according to the Scriptures "waiting" till His enemies are made the footstool of His feet; waiting till it pleases the Father to send Him once more, not as the Only Begotten, but as the First begotten from the dead into the inhabited earth (Heb. i:6.*)

In heaven in His own presence, as stated before, are the waiting multitudes of the redeemed, waiting for the fulness of redemption. On earth is His waiting Church composed of those who are born again. They are waiting for that promised glory, His glory so graciously to be shared by all His own. We shall now follow the most thrilling part of, "The Hope of the Ages," which is still unrealized, but which looms now so large on the horizon of our significant times.

---

*In Hebrews i:6-ii:5, the word "world" in the Greek is not *kosmos*, the physical world. Nor is it "aion," an age. It is *oikumine*, the inhabited earth.

CHAPTER IV

Hundreds of Questions. But Only One Answer

The Bible, God's holy and infallible Word, is the great book of hope and assurance. It reveals the brightest and most glorious future for humanity. Its optimistic predictions and visions are of such a nature that they could not have originated in the finite mind of man. They are supernatural. The men who were used in transmitting them to mankind claimed that they were not the productions of their own minds, but that they were received by them. This is demonstrated by such phrases, found hundreds of times in the Bible, as "Thus saith the Lord"; "The Word of the Lord came unto me"; "The Lord said"; "The Spirit of the Lord came unto me." These and other statements cannot mean anything but divine revelation. In these visions and promises of hope a sovereign voice is heard. Thousands of times that voice says, "*It shall be*"! These supernatural assurances of righteousness, peace, blessing, and glory concern the entire human race. Jews and Gentiles are promised a wonderful future. A part of Judaism has always clung tenaciously to these promises. True it is a majority has abandoned the promises of their own prophets and cast themselves into the arms of rationalism. But there is still a large number of Bible believing Jews who wait for the accomplishment of the hope of Israel. They still breathe out the age-long sigh of their fathers: "O, that the salvation of Israel were come out of Zion! When God bringeth back the captivity of His people, Jacob shall rejoice, and Israel shall be glad" (Psa. liii:6). They still wait for the promise: "And the Redeemer shall come out of Zion" (Isa. lix:20). Gentiles too wait for what is promised to them. Christendom, at least the greater part, expects that some day these promises of hope and universal blessing will come to pass, and the dawn of a better day will arrive. Furthermore, the Bible holds out a hope for all creation. Therefore we call the Bible the great Book of Hope. What a hopeless world it would be if there were no Bible!

We shall now ask a number of questions relating to these promises and the great hope the Bible proclaims and later give the one answer which answers them all.

I. *As to the People Israel.*   Did Israel ever possess the land in the dimensions as promised to Abraham in a solemn covenant? (Gen. xv:18-21.)   Their world-wide dispersion was divinely announced many centuries before it ever took place.   It was and it is still a literal dispersion.   Moses and many of the Prophets announced this dispersion and described the sufferings, persecutions and tribulations which should be their portion.   Have these prophecies been fulfilled in many of their generations?   History answers affirmatively.   But have the many promises of regathering and national restoration found their fulfilment also?   We quote but a few: "The Lord thy God will turn thy captivity, and have compassion on thee, and will return and gather thee from all the nations, whither the Lord thy God hath scattered thee" (Deut. xxx:3).   When and how was this promise fulfilled?   There is a prophetic thanksgiving written in the one hundred and seventh Psalm for a future regathering of the dispersed nation, "out of all lands, from the east, and from the west, from the north and from the south"; has this taken place in history?   Isaiah has been called "the great evangel"; but he is pre-eminently the prophet of Israel's hope.   We shall quote but one passage: "And it shall come to pass in that day, that the Lord shall set His hand again the *second time* to recover the remnant of His people, which shall be left from Assyria, and from Egypt, and from Pathros, and from Cush, and from Elam, and from Shinar, and from Hamath, and from the islands of the sea.   And He shall set up an ensign for the nations, and shall assemble the outcasts of Israel, and gather together the dispersed of Judah from *the four corners of the earth*" (Isa. xi:11-12).   The *first time* a remnant returned from the Babylonian captivity, but here is another return promised from a far greater territory, from the four corners of the earth.   Has this ever happened? Jeremiah announced the same hope.

"Therefore, behold, the days come, saith the Lord that it

shall no more be said, The Lord liveth, that brought up the
children of Israel out of the land of Egypt; but the Lord
liveth, that brought up the children of Israel from the land
of the north, and from all the lands whither He had driven
them, and I will bring them again into their land that I
gave unto their fathers. Behold I will send for many
fishers, saith the Lord, and they shall fish them; and after
will I send many hunters, and they shall hunt them from
every mountain, and from every hill, and out of the holes
of the rock" (Jer. xvi:15-16). When has this taken place?
We know that an unbalanced method of Bible exegesis takes
a passage like this and applies it to "the Church," calling
it a spiritual Israel. Any intelligent person must see at
once that it can only mean the *literal* Israel. Many other
restoration promises are found in Jeremiah. We quote one
more: "Hear the word of the Lord, O ye nations, and
declare it in the isles afar off, and say, He that scattered
Israel will gather him, and keep him, as a shepherd doth his
flock" (Jer. xxxi:10). When has this promise been kept?
We listen to Ezekiel. "For thus saith Jehovah God; Behold, I, even I, will both search My sheep, and seek them
out. . . . And I will bring them out from the people and
gather them from the countries, and will bring them to their
own land, and feed them upon the mountains of Israel by
the rivers and in all inhabited places of the country" (Ezek.
xxxiv:14). The context shows it is a future gathering. Has
it taken place? "For I will take you from among the nations,
and gather you out of all countries, and will bring you into
your own land. Then will I sprinkle clean water upon you,
and ye shall be clean, from all your filthiness, and from all
your idols will I cleanse you. A new heart also will I give
you, and a new spirit will I put within you; and I will take
away the stony heart out of your flesh, and I will give you
a heart of flesh . . . and ye shall dwell in the land that I
gave to your fathers and ye shall be My people, and I will
be your God" (Ezek. xxxvi:24-38). It is a piece of folly
to go to this prophecy of Ezekiel to establish from it, as it
has been done, the correct mode of baptism as sprinkling.

Ezekiel's prophecy has nothing to do with baptism nor with the Church. Has this cleansing of Israel taken place? When in history had Israel as a nation a new birth to fit them to enter into the kingdom?

Hosea speaks of a future repentance of Israel. He records their words and their hope. "Come, and let us return unto the Lord; for He hath torn, and He will heal us; He hath smitten and He will bind us up. After two days He will revive us, on the third day He will raise us up, and we shall live in His sight" (Hos. vi:1-2). When did Israel's national and spiritual resurrection take place? The great seer of the day of the Lord, Joel, gives the future experiences of Israel and Jerusalem, besieged by a Northern army, from which the Lord will deliver them (chapter ii). This is followed by "the outpouring of the Spirit of God upon all flesh" with signs and wonders in the heavens and in the earth. Has Israel ever had such an experience? Was there ever in history a siege of Jerusalem corresponding to the siege prophesied by Joel? Pentecostalism, unscripturally, claims a fulfilment of the outpouring of the Spirit, but it is a mere delusion. All remains to be fulfilled.

Amos, the herdsman and gatherer of sycamore figs, adds his testimony given to him by the Lord: "In that day will I raise up the tabernacle of David that is fallen, and close up the breaches thereof; and I will raise up its ruins, and I will build it as in the days of old. . . . And I will bring again the captivity of My people Israel, and they shall build the waste cities, and inhabit them; and they shall plant vineyards, and drink the wine thereof, they shall also make gardens, and eat the fruit thereof. And I will plant them upon their land, and they shall *no more* be pulled out of their land which I have given them, saith Jehovah thy God" (Amos ix:11-15). Has David's kingdom been restored and when? Where is it today? Certainly *not* in Great Britain, as claimed by Anglo-Israelism. Micah, like his great contemporary, the prophet Isaiah, reveals a kingdom of peace, of world peace, with Jerusalem as its capital. Then, "They shall sit every man under his vine and under his fig tree; and none shall make them afraid, for the mouth of the Lord of hosts hath spoken it" (Micah iv:1-4). Can anyone tell us where we find such a kingdom now, or in the past history of our age? We listen to the charming and joyful words of Zephaniah: "Sing, O daughter of Zion; shout O Israel; be glad and rejoice with all thy heart, O daughter of Jerusalem. The Lord hath taken away thy judgments, He hath cast out thine enemies; the King of Israel, even Jehovah, is in the midst of thee, thou shalt not see evil any more. In that day it shall be said to Jerusalem, Fear thou not, and to Zion, Let not thine hands be slack. Jehovah thy God in the midst of thee is mighty, He will save, He will rejoice over thee with joy; He will rest in His love, He will joy over thee with singing" (Zeph. iii:14-17). Here is a double joy, the joy of Zion, of Israel and Jerusalem rejoicing because Heaven's King of Glory is in the midst of her. And He Himself, Jehovah, the King of Israel, rejoices over the remnant of His people whom He hath redeemed. Has such rejoicing taken place? Is He in the midst of Israel? Here again the spiritualizer, the allegorist, tells us it should all be applied to the Church and must be understood in a spiritual sense, but at best it makes nothing but nonsense, to do this. Haggai, like Ezekiel, speaks of another temple in Jerusalem which shall be filled with the Glory of the Lord. "The glory of this latter house shall be greater than of the former, saith the Lord of Hosts; and in this place I will give peace, saith the Lord of Hosts" (Hag. ii:9). Can some historian tell us how this promise has found its fulfilment? Zechariah, the greatest of the post-exilic prophets, surely did not prophesy of a return from the Babylonian captivity, for that had taken place. When were the following words of hope and glory fulfilled: "Sing and rejoice, O daughter of Zion, for, lo, I come, and I will dwell in the midst of thee, saith the Lord. And many nations shall be joined unto the Lord in that day, and shall be My people; and I will dwell in the midst of thee, and thou shalt know that the Lord of Hosts hath sent Me to thee"? (Zech. ii:10, 11.) Here is first a rejoicing daughter of Zion, the saved remnant of Israel; Jehovah is in their midst; many nations are joined in that day to the Lord. Again we ask, when has it been fulfilled? Here is another remarkable prophecy. "Thus saith the Lord of Hosts, In those days it shall come to pass, that ten men shall take hold out of all languages of the nations, even shall take hold of the skirt of him that is a Jew, saying, We will go with you, for we have heard that God is with you" (Zech. viii:23). When did this come to pass?

"And I will pour upon the house of David, and upon the inhabitants of Jerusalem the spirit of grace and supplications; and they shall look upon Me whom they have pierced, and shall mourn for Him as one mourneth for his only son, and shall be in bitterness of Him, as one that is in bitterness for his firstborn" (Zech. xii:10). There can be no question, the pierced One is the same person whose voice is heard in the twenty-second Psalm: "They pierced my hands and my feet." But when did the house of David and the inhabitants of Jerusalem ever make a national confession on account of the pierced One as demanded by the context of this prophecy? In the final chapter of Zechariah we find another prophecy about a great siege of Jerusalem. All nations are seen gathered against Jerusalem. But that siege will be interrupted, for the Lord will enter this fight and oppose the besieging nations. Furthermore Jehovah will be there in person and it is written, "His feet shall stand in that day upon the Mount of Olives and the Mount of Olives shall cleave in the midst thereof." Finally at the same time, "Jehovah my God shall come and all the saints with Thee" (Zech. xiv:1-5). Will some Bible scholar tell us when this remarkable siege took place and when Jerusalem was delivered by the manifestation of Jehovah bringing all His saints with Him?

Again we read; "And Jehovah shall be king over all the earth; in that day shall there be one Lord, and His name one" (Zech. xiv:9). When in past history was this true? Is it true today? *When* has idolatry been completely abolished, so that only the one Lord is worshiped?

Let it be remembered that we quote only a few of the large number of promises of a prophetic character, which demand not a spiritual, but a *literal* fulfilment, which have never been fulfilled, which are not now in process of fulfilment. That Jehovah-God promised to David a kingdom of world-wide dimensions, with Jerusalem as its earthly center, that a Son of David is to occupy the throne, is beyond the shadow of a doubt. The covenant made with David is, like the Abrahamic covenant, oath-bound. God's gifts and calling are without repentance. But when in past history was this kingdom established on earth? Here is one of the most outstanding texts. "Behold, the days come, saith the Lord, that I will raise unto David a righteous Branch, and a King shall reign and prosper, and shall execute judgment and justice on earth. In His days Judah shall be saved, and Israel shall dwell safely, and this is His name whereby He shall be called, The Lord our Righteousness" (Jer. xxiii:5, 6). Did such a king ever reign on earth? Is all Israel, the house of Judah and the house of Israel enjoying perfect safety as promised in the text? Current history furnishes the answer. Millions of Jews are the football of certain nations, kicked about from nation to nation, and darker clouds of a disastrous tribulation are now hanging over them. Here is another blessed prophetic promise relating to the time of that promised kingdom, "Break forth into joy, sing together, ye waste places of Jerusalem, for Jehovah has comforted His people, He hath redeemed Jerusalem. Jehovah hath made bare His holy arm in the eyes of all nations; and all the ends of the earth shall see the salvation of our God" (Isa. lii:9, 10). We cannot locate the fulfilment of this prophecy. In another portion (chapter 60) Isaiah beholds Gentile nations and their kings gathering to Jerusalem. "And the sons of strangers shall build up thy walls, and their kings shall minister unto thee. For in My wrath I smote thee, but in My favour I had mercy on thee. Therefore thy gates shall be open continually; they shall not be shut day or night; that men may bring unto thee the forces of the Gentiles. . . . The sons also of them that afflicted thee shall come bending unto thee; and all they that despised thee shall bow themselves down at the soles of thy feet; and they shall call thee, the City of the Lord, the Zion of the Holy One of Israel.   Whereas thou hast been forsaken and hated, so that no man went through thee, I will make thee an eternal excellency, a joy of many generations.   .   .   .   Violence shall no more be heard in thy land, wasting nor destruction within thy borders; but thou shalt call thy walls Salvation, and thy gates Praise" (Isa. lx:10-22).   The unprecedented antisemitism of our times and the struggles of the Zionists in Palestine show that this prophecy of comfort is still unrealized.   How many more of such prophetic promises as to Jerusalem we could add!

Ezekiel, too, beheld the final struggles in Palestine and described the invasion of Gog and Magog and their defeat (Chapters 38, 39).   That this invasion is still in the future may be learned from the closing verse of the thirty-ninth chapter of Ezekiel.   "Neither will I hide My face any more from them; for I have poured out My Spirit upon the house of Israel, saith Jehovah God."

And then the vision of that great Temple, which follows the overthrow of the enemies of Israel!   Expositors have unsuccessfully attempted to explain this vision.   Others left it severely alone.   It cannot be possibly applied to the Church.   The only way of explanation is to accept the literal meaning of a literal Temple to be erected in Jerusalem (Ezek. 40-46).   The Lord and His glory will enter into that Temple.   Has there ever been such a Temple?   Most significantly Ezekiel ends his prophecy with a description of Jerusalem, not a heavenly, but an earthly city, with its gates.   No longer will Jerusalem be called by its old name alone.   It will receive a new name: *"Jehovah Shammah"*— the Lord is there.   Jerusalem has never been known by that name.

II.   As to the Gentile Nations.   A difference is made in the Word of God between Israel, which means the natural descendants of the twelve sons of Jacob, and the other nations.   Balaam had to utter this truth, though against his will. "Lo, the people (Israel) shall dwell alone, and shall not be reckoned among the nations" (Num. xxiii:9). The Hebrew word *"Gojim"* has generally been translated in the King James version, as well as others, by the word "heathen"; the better rendering is "nations", including other semitic races; the offspring of Ham and of Japheth. Their origin and the origin of the various religious systems such as Confucianism, Brahmanism, Zoroastrianism, as well as Polytheism, the author has treated in two other volumes*.

All the nations of the world, including the most degenerate cannibals and others have also promises of blessing, of righteousness and peace and prosperity. The Word of God proclaims a wonderful future for them. We shall quote a limited number of the prophetic promises of hope which belong to all the nations of the earth.

Moses in his great prophetic song, in which his own nation's past, present, and future are so startlingly revealed, mentions in the final stanza the nations. "Rejoice, O ye nations, with His people (Israel), for He will avenge the blood of His servants, and will render vengeance to His adversaries, and will be merciful unto His land, and to His people" (Deut. xxxii:43). Has such a time of rejoicing taken place at any time during the course of our present age? Is there anything like it in sight today? Has God dealt with the enemies of His people? But we must notice that the rejoicing of the nations with His people Israel is linked to the mercy shown to Israel and Israel's land. So there can be no rejoicing of nations till the adversaries are judged and Israel has received her promised blessings of mercy.

The nations are prominently mentioned in a brief but very comprehensive Psalm of David, the second Psalm. It starts with a prophecy of revolting, raging nations. It may well be termed, world revolution. Kings and rulers, the nations and the people (Israel) are opposing God's Anointed; they strive hard to get rid of all divine restraints. It is a picture of our own times as our age draws rapidly to its pre-

---

*"Christianity or Religion": and "As it was,—so shall it be."

dicted and appointed end. But suddenly the scene changes.
Kings, rulers, whatever they are called, presidents or dictators, are dethroned and one great King is enthroned. He
fills Zion's throne. Has the day of His crowning taken
place? This King is to have a great inheritance. God
promises Him the nations and the uttermost parts of the
earth for His possession. Needless to say no such king has
ever reigned to whom the crown rights of all nations are
divinely given. The rule of that King of all nations is more
fully described in another great prophetic Psalm, the seventy-
second. He is going to be a righteous judge. He is going
to judge the poor, save the children of the needy and break
in pieces the oppressor. He shall have dominion from sea
to sea, unto the ends of the earth. All nations, none excepted,
shall serve that King. All nations will worship Him and
praise Him. The whole earth is to be filled with His glory.
But in what century since this Psalm was written, three
thousand years ago, has there been such a king, or such a
kingdom of righteousness and peace and glory?

Isaiah's great vision concerning the nations we quote in
full: "And it shall come to pass in the last days, that the
mountain of the Lord's house shall be established in the top
of the mountains, and shall be exalted above the hills; and
all nations shall flow unto it. And many people shall go
and say, Come ye, and let us go up to the mountain of the
Lord, to the house of the God of Jacob; and He will teach
us of His ways, and we will walk in His paths; for out of
Zion shall go forth the law, and the Word of the Lord from
Jerusalem. And He shall judge among the nations, and
shall rebuke many people, and they shall beat their swords
into plowshares, and their spears into pruninghooks; nation
shall not lift up sword against nation, neither shall they
learn war any more" (Isa. ii:2-4).

That this prophecy has nothing to do with the Church is
obvious. Commentators claim that "the Lord's house" is
the church and that all nations will come into the Church.
They speak of Christian nations. But where are they? It
is sheer nonsense to claim that England, France, Italy,

Germany, Spain, and the smaller European nations are "Christian." Some even speak of Soviet Russia. Equally so is the United States, the most lawless country on the face of the earth, not a "Christian" country. When have nations ever turned swords into plowshares and spears into pruning-hooks? How and when will this prophecy become reality? Today it is the opposite. The implements of agriculture are turned into the weapons of war. Do the nations of today learn war no more? As never before these so-called "Christian" nations, *military Christendom*, prepare war by huge armament programs, which must plunge ere long these nations into wholesale murder on a gigantic scale, unknown in all history. That coming war of these nations, when it comes, will end our boasting twentieth century civilization. And so we ask again, when will the nations of the earth learn war no more? Micah, the contemporary of Isaiah, received the same vision adding a beautiful scene of peace (Micah iv:1-4). We have quoted before from Zechariah's vision that a day is coming "when many nations shall be joined to the Lord" (Zech. ii:11). Inasmuch as no nation as such was joined to the Lord in the past, nor in the present, it must come to pass in the future. In another great prophecy Zechariah sees nations under the reign of a great king, who speaks peace to them, a king who rules over all. "And I will cut off the chariot from Ephraim, and the horse from Jerusalem, and the battle bow shall be cut off. And He shall speak peace unto the nations; and His dominion shall be from sea to sea, and from the river even unto the ends of the earth" (Zech. ix:10). This prophecy is preceded by the coming of a king to Jerusalem. "Rejoice greatly, O daughter of Zion; shout O daughter of Jerusalem. Behold, thy King cometh unto thee, He is just, and having salvation; lowly, and riding upon an ass, and upon a colt the foal of an ass" (verse 9). Every Christian knows who this King is. Matthew xxi:4-5 shows its fulfilment. But has He ever spoken peace to the nations? Has He dominion from sea to sea? Another prophecy of universal peace is found in a prophetic Psalm. "He maketh wars to cease unto the end of the earth; He breaketh the bow, and cutteth the spear asunder; He burneth the chariot in the fire. Be still, and know that I am God. I will be exalted among the nations, I will be exalted in the earth" (Psa. xlvi:9, 10).

Is the Lord exalted among the nations of the earth today?

Another important question comes to us from a most wonderful prophecy in another Psalm. "The Lord said unto my Lord, Sit Thou at My right hand, until I make Thine enemies Thy footstool" (Psa. cx:1). Matthew xx:41-46 is a perfect comment on this verse. He who gives it is David's son and David's Lord, the promised seed, God manifested in the flesh. After His sacrificial death and triumphant resurrection, He ascended up on high, and after passing through the heavens He took His place at the right hand of God in the heaven of heavens. While He is exercising there His priestly ministry in behalf of His people, as well as His advocacy, He is also waiting. He is waiting till His enemies are made the footstool of His feet. His enemies, according to the second Psalm are the opposing nations, who refuse His authority, who are against God and against His Christ. His enemies are the different religious systems of heathendom many of them steeped in vile immoralities, the different forms of polytheism and fetishism as well as Islam. To these enemies of God and of His Christ we must add the cultured liberalism and the different schools of rationalism which flourish in Christendom. Behind all stand unseen enemies, Satan and the demon world and the fallen angels. Let us remember after Christ has waited well nigh two thousand years, the enemies which are to be made the footstool of His feet, flourish more than ever before in history. Look at the ever-increasing powerful "isms" in the political world—Socialism, Communism, Fascism and its little brother Nazism. They differ from each other. In one thing they agree, they are anti-God and anti-Christ. They aim at the destruction of the Church of Jesus Christ. Worse than the pagan Roman persecutions of the Church have been the Russian persecutions. Over two million people were murdered, hundreds upon hundreds of edifices have been destroyed, the most horrible blasphemies defying God have been uttered. The "Society of the Godless" continues its destructive work. In Spain the Reds, camouflaged under the name of "Loyalists," have murdered within two years several thousands of priests and other clerics, destroyed churches and religious institutions. In the land of Luther under the Hitler-Rosenberg regime the attempt is made to destroy true Christianity and to substitute for it an Aryan-Germanic counterfeit which is half pagan, and ignores both sin and the redemption which humanity needs.

What do we find in professing Christendom? Ritualism on one hand and Rationalism on the other. Look at what used to be called Protestantism! True enough there is a strong evangelical current, call it conservative or fundamental, a loyal element which keeps His Word and does not deny His Name. But they are in the minority and becoming more so each year. The denials of the great essentials of the Christian faith are prominent in universities, colleges, theological seminaries and in the leading religious journals. The Liberalists also known by the name of Modernists side openly with Socialism and Communism, call themselves "the Friends of the Soviets", endorse certain "Fronts", support the Red cause in Spain under the plea of democracy. Siding thus with the enemy they become partakers of their evil work. Christ rejection, the cry "we will not have this Man reign over us," was never as prominent as in 1938. And now comes our question. If Christ waits till His enemies are made the footstool of His feet, how long will He have to wait? If enmity against God and against His Christ increases constantly, who is going to end it? The youth of different countries are trained to take the road of atheism. Will the next generation submit more to God and accept His Word more than the present one? If heathendom increases every year by millions through a natural increase, how and when will the world be converted to God and to His Christ? According to Apostolic revelation

every knee is to bow at the name of Jesus and every tongue
is to confess His Lordship (Phil. ii).   When will it come?

Here is another great message of Isaiah. "And the
Gentiles shall come to thy light and kings to the brightness
of thy rising. Lift up thine eyes round about, and see;
all they gather themselves and come together, they come to
thee; thy sons shall come from afar, and thy daughters
shall be nursed at thy side . . .   the forces of the
Gentiles shall come unto thee   . . .   they shall show
forth the praises of the Lord" (Isa. lx:1-6). Has the world
ever seen such a gathering?

In numerous prophetic Psalms the rejoicing and the
worship of the nations of the earth is foretold. They
predict singing times for all the nations of the world. Think
of that forecast of the one hundredth Psalm, "Make a joyful
noise unto the Lord all ye lands. Serve the Lord with
gladness, come before His presence with singing" (Psa. c:1, 2).

Have all the lands of the earth ever made a joyful noise
unto the Lord? Or, has the character of nations ever been
changed from "hateful and hating each other"? (Titus
iii:3). Are they now singing "hymns of hate" or "hymns
of love and praise"? Many times we read in the Word of
God that the Lord will judge the nations in righteousness,
that the prevailing unrighteousness and injustice among the
nations will be forever abolished. "When Thy judgments
are in the earth, the inhabitants of the world will learn righteousness" (Isa. xxvi:9). Inasmuch as all nations are still
steeped in unrighteousness and injustice these judgments
have not been. When will they come? Joel had a great
vision of a judgment. "I will also gather all nations, and
will bring them down into the valley of Jehoshaphat, and
will plead with them there for My People and my heritage
Israel, whom they have scattered among the nations, and
parted My land" (Joel iii:2). Has God dealt with the
nations on account of their sins against His people Israel?
We refrain from quoting many other predictions concerning
the nations and the promises of hope when righteousness
reigns and peace on earth prevails.

III. *As to God's Creation.* It is a wonderful creation! The heavens declare the glory of God! Three thousand years ago a Spirit-endued Israelite wrote: "O Lord, how manifold are Thy works! in wisdom hast Thou made them all; the earth is full of Thy riches" (Psa. civ:24). In Revelation we read the purpose of creation: "Thou hast created all things, and for Thy pleasure they are and were created" (Rev. iv:11). What about the other side? Cyclones and tornadoes sweep over God's fair creation, working a terrible destruction. Earthquakes devastate many regions of different continents; volcanoes emit their streams of hot lava inflicting sufferings on man, beast, and vegetation. There are droughts and dust storms which turn the most fruitful lands into a hopeless wilderness. Ferocious animals attack man, poisonous snakes and insects claim many thousands of human victims. As we write we look in summer time at a number of stately trees. But they are completely stripped of all foliage, they look as they are in midwinter. Myriads of insects, worms, and caterpillars did this work in a few days. There is a terrible blight upon all creation. Did a kind and loving Creator create such things for His own pleasure and glory?

We must also look upon him who is God's supreme creation on earth, man, made a little lower than the angels. In the first chapter of this volume we stated that the creation of man in the image of God was an expression of His love. What is the condition of the race today? Misery upon misery! Increasing sufferings and afflictions! Disease upon disease! A never ending struggle for existence! Famines and pestilences claim millions of victims! Great floods sweep hundreds and thousands away. Man invents, scientists discover; but for what? Presumably to make life more livable; in reality to increase the curse and the misery of humanity. Take the much boasted aerial navigation. It is lauded as a great triumph. Look at China and its destroyed cities, its suffering millions! Look at Spain and the thousands of slaughtered women and children. Chemists invent and discover new explosives, new chemicals to satisfy the demands of the war-lord, the murderer from the beginning. Why is it thus? We have answered it before. The answer consists in three letters: S-I-N. But are these things to continue for ever and ever? If so, God would be a defeated God.

We listen again to the words of hope written in the Bible. "The wolf also shall dwell with the lamb, and the leopard shall lie down with the kid; and the calf and the young lion and the fatling together; and a little child shall lead them. And the cow and the bear shall feed; their young ones shall lie down together; and the lion shall eat straw like the ox. And the sucking child shall play on the hole of the asp, and the weaned child shall put his hand on the cockatrice' den. They shall not hurt nor destroy in all my holy mountain; for the earth shall be full of the knowledge of the Lord, as the waters cover the sea" (Isa. xi:6-9.) "Instead of the thorn shall come up the fir tree, and instead of the brier shall come up the myrtle tree" (Isa. lv:13). Who authorizes the expositor to say that these words have not a literal meaning but they must be understood allegorically and given a spiritual interpretation? But let us go to the glorious summit of the Roman epistle. Here we find a great inspired vision of the Apostle Paul. It concerns the hope of creation. "For the earnest expectation of the creature waiteth for the manifestation of the sons of God. For the creature was made subject to vanity, not willingly, but by reason of Him who hath subjected the same in hope. Because the creature itself also shall be delivered from the bondage of corruption into the glorious liberty of the children of God. For we know that the whole creation groaneth and travaileth in pain together until now" (Rom. viii:19-22). And so a time must come when creation's groans cease, when creation itself has its redemption day. But how and when? That is the question.

We have asked many questions as to these promises of hope. We could have filled three times as many pages with similar questions. We must now give attention to answer these questions. Will these prophecies of hope find some day their literal fulfilment or will history never record their realization? This is a serious question. The men used in giving these sayings and promises of hope declared solemnly that they were the mouthpieces of the Lord. The hope they hold out for humanity, for Jew and Gentile and creation, did not spring from their own brains; all came to them from a supernatural source. Hence if there never comes a fulfilment it would mean that the prophets were self-deceived, deceivers perhaps, dreamers or fanatics. If such is the case then we must close the book we have termed the Book of books, discard it, and abandon every promise as a false hope and stare hopelessly into an enigmatical future with no ray of light. Perish the thought! Such will never be the case. There is a great evidence that these men were not dreamers, fanatics, deceivers or self-deceived. That evidence is fulfilled prophecy. Scores of prophetic utterances these same men made have found their literal fulfilment, prophecies apart from those relating to Christ, our Saviour, and His sufferings. Fulfilled prophecy therefore vouches for the literal fulfilment of the unfulfilled promises of hope and glory.

But what is the answer to the questions we have asked? When and how is the glorious future of Israel to become true, when and how will their sufferings end? When and how will a great world-wide Kingdom be set up? When and how will nations learn war no more and live in a great universal brotherhood? When and how will righteousness and peace kiss each other? When and how will the whole world rejoice in the loving kindness of their Creator-God, worship Him who paid for it all by the shedding of His blood? When and how will all the world acknowledge Him as King of kings and Lord of lords? When and how will every evil be banished and every false religion from low down Fetishism to the philosophical babblings of Buddhism and others be abolished? When and how will the modern atheism of science, falsely so-called, be silenced forever and the Anti-christianity in cap and gown, flourishing in Christendom today, be no more? When and how will the curse of sin be removed from God's fair creation?

Can man bring it all about by his endeavors? Can the Jews fulfill their prophecies of restoration by political Zionism? Can they restore themselves? Can the remnants of the ten tribes, the so-called lost tribes, though they are not lost, find their way back to their land? Can political schemes stop Antisemitism? Can political "isms" be arrested by united fronts? Is the professing Church on earth to meddle in political schemes and by the Babylon spirit of federation bring about better religious and moral conditions? Will the Church succeed in her unscriptural attempt to convert the whole world and bring all nations to the feet of Christ? Will the Church succeed in the complete abolishment of Atheism, Antichristianity and all other false beliefs? Will pacifism, as sponsored through communistic propaganda in our institutions of learning, end all wars? Can four or five, or six, or ten power pacts bring about peace on earth? Can flood controls arrest cloudbursts? Can seismographs stop earthquakes? Can science stop tornadoes and cyclones, famines and pestilences? Can serums cure every disease? Will science do away with cemeteries? And how many more questions we might ask, yet every question would have to be answered with NO!

There is but one answer to all these questions concerning the promised hope for Israel, for the nations of the earth and for all creation. That answer is:

The Lord Jesus Christ.

He alone is the only answer, the completest answer, the never-failing answer to all our questions. But what do we mean when we give His ever blessed and adorable Name, the Name above every other name, as the only answer? We do not mean that the answer is a practical application of the principles of righteousness declared by the infallible teacher in the sermon on the mount. We do not mean the practise of what has been termed the golden rule. We do not mean a leadership of Jesus. We do not mean that these questions will be answered by future spiritual revivals, nor do we mean that a blasted Western civilization, misnamed Christian, will influence heathen nations to accept Christianity and turn to God from their idols. The sorrowful fact is that what military Christendom has done and is doing, and the shameful failures of Western civilization, has been a curse to heathen nations.

What we mean, the only answer, the completest and never-failing answer to all our questions, is

The Glorious Reappearing of the Lord Jesus Christ.

This future event will answer every question, solve every problem which humanity faces today, and all the existing chaotic conditions, and bring about that golden age of which heathen poets dreamed, which the Bible promises is in store for the earth. He appeared once at the end of the age, the Jewish age, "to put away sin by sacrifice of Himself." Immediately after this statement we read that "*He shall appear the second time*" (Heb. ix:26-28). For a universal judgment, a universal resurrection, the end of all things? No! He shall appear *unto salvation*. Redemption and salvation are twofold according to the Word of God, by Blood and by Power. Redemption by Blood was the object of His first coming, as the seed of the woman, in humiliation, to suffer and to die. That work is finished and is now and for ever the only hope for lost humanity. The message which is sent forth, the great message for this age, is the message of salvation. Its appeal and promise is, "Whosoever believeth in Him shall not perish but have everlasting life." All who accept and are saved become the members of His mystical body, the Church.

But Redemption by Blood, His finished work on the Cross, is the basis of Redemption by Power. That power will not be displayed till the purpose of our age, the out-calling of a people for His Name, is accomplished. It will be manifested when He who is in His glorified human body at the right hand of God, returns once more in great power and glory. Then His power in salvation, His power over His enemies, His power as omnipotent Creator-Redeemer, will be fully demonstrated. The heel will crush the serpent's head.

The national hope of Israel, their spiritual regeneration, their long promised restoration, the defeat of their enemies, the establishment of the world-wide kingdom, the supremacy and glory of the earthly Jerusalem, the house of the Lord in the top of the mountains, the law and the Word of the Lord going forth from there, all is dependent on the reappearing of the Lord Jesus Christ. He is the King who will be enthroned upon the holy hill of Zion, the King, who shall reign and prosper, the King, whose name is, "the Lord our righteousness," who receives the nations for His inheritance and the uttermost parts of the earth for His possession. The great King described in that great prophetic Psalm, which marked the end of the prayers of David (Psa. lxxii) is the Virgin-born Son of God of the seed of David. He will execute the judgments and rule in righteousness. With redemption power He will break in pieces the oppressor, dictators, all enemies, the wicked, the lawless and the great leaders of the end-time, the little horn of Daniel's vision (Dan. vii), and the man of sin, the son of perdition, the final antichrist. He is the King who will have dominion from sea to sea, unto the ends of the earth, the King whom all nations shall call blessed. He is also the Prince of Peace. He will bring not only peace, but abundance of peace (Psa. lxxii:7).

By His power He will make wars to cease and will change all swords into plowshares and spears into pruninghooks. All cannot be till the day of His return appears. All is conditioned by His personal and glorious return, the return which the prisoner in Babylon so vividly beheld. "And I saw in the night visions, behold, one like the Son of Man came with the clouds of heaven, and came to the ancient of days, and they brought Him near before Him, And there was given Him dominion, and glory, and a kingdom, that all people, nations, and languages, should serve Him. His dominion is an everlasting dominion, which shall not pass away, and His kingdom which shall not be destroyed" (Dan. vii:13-14). It is then when not civilization, or modern progress, or the Church, or spiritual revivals down all His enemies to be the footstool of His feet, but when God does it what He promised to Him, "I will make Thine enemies Thy footstool." Then begins His reign, when all things are put in subjection under His feet (Heb. ii:8). Nineteen hundred years ago the inspired pen of the writer of the Hebrew Epistle wrote, "But now we see not yet all things put under Him." This is as true in 1938 as it was when first written. Nor will there come a change till He comes back to earth again and receives the promised throne, the throne of His father David (Luke i:32). "At that time they shall call Jerusalem the throne of the Lord; and all the nations shall be gathered into it, to the name of the Lord, to Jerusalem; neither shall they walk any more after the imagination of their evil heart" (Jer. iii:17).

Only after His return and enthronement will nations break forth in singing, as they know Him as King of kings and Lord of lords. Rejoicing in all the earth cannot come till He reigns. "The Lord reigneth; let the earth rejoice; let the multitudes of the isles be glad" (Psa. xcvii:1). How plainly it is all revealed in Scripture! The age ends with a time of great trouble, a great tribulation (Dan. xii:1-2; Matt. xxiv:21). It will be "the day of calamity" for Israel (Deut. xxxii:35), the time of Jacob's trouble (Jer. xxx:7). Against Jerusalem comes the Northern Army (Joel ii); the siege of Jerusalem (Zech. xiv) takes place. In Jerusalem in a temple the abomination of desolation is in power, the man of sin, Israel's false Messiah, will be there and is worshipped by apostate Israel, while Israel's faithful remnant suffers and waits patiently for the Redeemer to come to Zion. Their hopes do not miscarry. Perhaps while they are praying, "O that Thou wouldest rend the heavens, that Thou wouldest come down, that the mountains might flow down at Thy presence" (Isa. lxiv:1), the sun in the sky suddenly is darkened, it is eclipsed by a greater sun, the Sun of Righteousness. There up in the sky a light and glory-flashing cloud appears, and upon it "one like unto the Son of Man." Wild consternation prevails everywhere, fear and trembling sweep over all, but Israel's remnant and with them Gentiles who accepted their testimony in faith and repentance, when the powers of heaven are shaken, know that their redemption draweth nigh (Luke xxi:25-28). They break forth in rejoicing and praise—"Lo, this is our God; we have waited for Him, and He will save us; this is the Lord; we have waited for Him, we will be glad and rejoice in His salvation" (Isa. xxv:9). Then judgments follow, nations are judged, the unseen powers headed by the old serpent, Satan, the devil, the dragon, will be imprisoned and after that comes His glorious reign.

This wonderful program of God for Israel and the nations is tersely stated in a Psalm. "O sing unto the Lord a new song; for He hath done marvelous things; His right hand, and His holy arm, hath gotten Him the victory. The Lord hath made known His salvation; His righteousness hath He shown openly in the sight of the nations. He hath remembered His mercy and His truth toward the house of Israel; all the ends of the earth have seen the salvation of our God. Make a joyful noise unto the Lord, all the earth, make a loud noise, and rejoice, and sing praise" (Psa. xcviii:1-4). Read also Psalm cii:13-22. The nations shall fear the name of the Lord, and all the kings His glory. It comes when the Lord builds up Zion, the only true Zion in the world, the Zion of Israel. But when does He build Zion and the tabernacle of David? "When the Lord shall build Zion, He shall appear in His glory."

And gaze upon Him once more, the Christ of suffering, sin and curse bearing! They platted a crown of thorns and pressed it upon His noble brow. It must have remained there, till His thorn-crowned head, after the victorious shout, sank on His breast. That crown of thorns is emblematic of creation's curse. Not science with its inventions and discoveries can arrest or even ameliorate the curse of sin. Only One can remove it. He is Creation's Lord who paid the price of redemption and whose redemption power can alone deliver groaning creation. But it will never come till He comes again, no longer wearing the crown of mockery, but crowned with many diadems. According to Paul groaning creation waits for deliverance and that will come with "the manifestation of the sons of God." The latter will not take place till He appears and all His saints with Him.

And so we say it again, the answer to every question we ask as to the fulfilment of unfulfilled prophecy is the return of our Redeemer-Lord, the Head of the Church, the Lord of Glory and Israel's King, the King of kings and Lord of lords. His second coming, His glorious manifestation, is the great hope, *the only hope*, for all the earth. When it comes, and it will surely come, it will be the greatest event in human history next to the Cross. It will usher in the age of righteousness, peace and glory, so wonderfully great that it will surpass all our expectations. All waits for that coming event.

CHAPTER V

His Own Testimony

We hear someone saying, after having read the previous chapter: "What you have written is merely a theory, representing the literal interpretation of prophecy, but there is another side which is endorsed by a majority of Christians. How can we know which is the right interpretation?" There is a very simple answer to this question. The Lord Jesus Christ came from heaven to earth as the Prophet of God, He came to reveal God and to make known the Truth of God. He came to teach. Nicodemus said to Him: "Rabbi, we know that Thou art a teacher come from God." As not only come from God, sent by the Father, but as God Himself He is the highest and the final authority as to revelation and the interpretation of prophecy. We must therefore examine His own prophetic teachings as found in the records of the Gospel, primarily in the synoptic Gospels. We find in these teachings many allusions to the leading prophecies of the Old Testament. More than that, He has given us a good key. Which shall we accept, His own testimony, or the testimony and interpretation of theologians or systems of theology? No true believer in our Lord will hesitate a moment in answering this question.

We have mentioned before a great fundamental passage of the Roman Epistle which we must now examine in its important meaning.

"Now I say this that Jesus Christ was a minister of the circumcision for the Truth of God, to confirm the promises made unto the fathers; and that the Gentiles might glorify God for His mercy; as it is written, for this cause will I confess Thee among the Gentiles, and sing unto Thy name. And again He saith, Rejoice ye Gentiles with His people. And again, Praise the Lord, all ye Gentiles, and laud Him, all ye people. And again, Isaiah saith, There shall be a root of Jesse, and He that shall rise to reign over theGentiles; in Him shall the Gentiles trust" (Rom. xv:8-12). It is a great prophetic declaration which has been overlooked by many Bible teachers. Here we read that our Lord in His earthly ministry was a minister of the circumcision. His ministry was confined to Israel. The synoptic Gospels, especially Matthew, record this exclusive ministry. As we have seen when He came in humiliation, when He came to put away sin by the sacrifice of Himself, all those promises relating to His sacrificial work were literally accomplished. But are these all the promises made unto the fathers in the Old Testament prophetic Word? A careful examination of Old Testament Prophecy will prove our assertion that, as we have already demonstrated in this volume, the vast majority of prophetic promises remain unfulfilled. These relate to His Kingship and the earthly Kingdom and the blessings and glory connected with both. Let us notice that the quoted passage states that He came to *confirm* these promises, not to *fulfil* them. And if these promises were not fulfilled, but only confirmed, when He was on earth, they must then be fulfilled in the future. In our preceding chapter we showed that all these promises of hope and glory are linked to the re-appearing, the second coming of our Lord, their fulfilment therefore necessitates His personal and glorious return. But how could these promises be confirmed if He had not come first of all as the promised King to Israel? When He came finally, at the close of His three years ministry to Jerusalem, immediately before His passion, it is written, that, "All this was done, that it might be fulfilled which was spoken by the Prophet, Tell ye the daughter of Zion, Behold, *Thy King* cometh unto thee, meek, and sitting upon an ass, and the colt, the foal of an ass" (Matt. xxi:4, 5). An examination of this quotation from the Prophet Zechariah (Chapter ix) shows that certain statements are omitted by Matthew, for these could not be fulfilled when He was presented to Jerusalem as the Messiah-King. His preaching and teaching in His ministry up to a certain time, concerned that promised kingdom. The great message was, "The Kingdom of the heavens is at hand." He confirmed this message by the signs and powers of the Kingdom. Yet it also had been revealed through the prophets that His own, Israel, would reject Him, and that the promised Kingdom would be given to Christ when He comes in the clouds of heaven. Furthermore in the great prophecy in the ninth chapter of Daniel it is clearly stated that "Messiah should be cut off and have nothing," that is, no kingdom (Dan. ix:26, correct translation).

The reference to the Gentiles in the quoted passage is equally interesting and instructive. We read first, "That the Gentiles might glorify God for His mercy; as it is written, for this cause I will confess thee among the Gentiles and sing unto Thy name" (Psa. lvii:9 compare with Psa. xxii:22). This evidently means that after our Lord had confirmed the promises made unto the fathers, and after His rejection, mercy would go forth to the Gentiles. "And it shall come to pass, that in the place where it was said unto them, Ye are not my people, there it shall be said unto them, ye are the sons of the living God" (Hos. i:10). Or, as it is stated in Romans, "Ye (Gentiles) in times past have not believed God, yet have now obtained mercy through their (Israel's) unbelief" (Rom. xi:30). "Through their fall salvation is come to the Gentiles."

The other quoted passages relating to the Gentiles are *unfulfilled.* They will be fulfilled with the return of Christ.

But let us see how the Lord in His earthly ministry confirmed the prophetic promises of the Old Testament. He did more than that; He has given us an interpretation and furnished us the key to their right understanding. His confirmation and interpretation should deliver every true Christian from the unscriptural invention that the Kingdom is only a spiritual Kingdom, that the unfulfilled promises must be "spiritualized" till they disappear in the haze and thickening mists of allegorization and modernistic denial.

One of the outstanding prophetic books is the Book of Daniel. In it we find a remarkable forecast of the political history of that period of time, which our Lord calls, "The Times of the Gentiles." Linked with this forecast is the future history of Israel and the dawn of the kingdom age. The final events in store for Israel, when the present age closes, are found in the second half of the eighth chapter, in chapter xi:25-27 and in xi:36-45 and the twelfth chapter. On account of these startling predictions this great book has been severely attacked by the rationalistic enemies of the Word of God. But God has seen to its vindication. Nowhere has the defeat of the destructive critics been so marked as on this battlefield over the authenticity of the Book of Daniel.

To give the history of this remarkable vindication would fill scores of pages.* The modernistic echoes who still repeat the exploded arguments against Daniel are decidedly out of date. Truth lives always, but error dies hard. What Daniel reveals about the future is the stumblingblock for the liberalists in Christendom. We shall see how our Lord, the infallible Teacher, confirms some of Daniel's prophecies and also their correct interpretations.

The first great prophetic chapter is the second chapter. Indeed it is one of the great pivotal chapters of the entire Bible and unless a Christian understands this chapter correctly he must be at sea in all prophecy. As we have given in our "World Prospects" and our "Exposition of Daniel" the meaning of Nebuchadnezzar's prophetic dream we do not enlarge upon it here. That dream-image spans the entire times of the Gentiles, beginning with Nebuchadnezzar the golden head, to the end of the times of the Gentiles, when the extinct Roman Empire will be revived and appear in its final form composed of clay governments and the ten kings, domineered over by a great dictator, seen as a little horn in the seventh chapter.

What interests us most is the catastrophic ending of the times of the Gentiles. In the dream is seen a stone falling out of heaven and striking the clay feet of the image with its little iron toes, pulverizing the whole image. Then suddenly the smiting stone becomes a mountain filling the whole earth. All kinds of interpretations of that smiting stone have been given. Some say the stone represents Christ in His first coming and the smiting began when He was on

---

*"Read The Book of Daniel," by the writer. A complete exposition.

earth. That it has been going on all along; the smiting is done by the Gospel and civilization, and gradually His kingdom grows till finally it fills the whole earth. What liberty these expositors take with the Word of God! The text does not teach that there is a gradual striking of the stone and that it will take several thousand years for that stone to become a mountain. It is *one sudden, decisive blow,* and the smiting stone becomes a mountain. Perhaps the most ludicrous explanation is the one made by British Israelism. They teach that the smiting stone represents Great Britain.

But let us listen to the words of the Lord Jesus. "Jesus saith unto them, Did ye never read in the Scriptures, the stone which the builders rejected, the same is become the head of the corner; this is the Lord's doing, and it is marvelous in our eyes. Therefore I say unto you, The kingdom of God shall be taken from you, and given to a nation bringing forth the fruit thereof. And whosoever shall fall on that stone shall be broken; but on whomsoever it shall fall, it will grind him to powder" (Matt. xxi:42, 44). He teaches that He Himself is the stone (Gen. xlix:24). He would be for Israel the stone of stumbling and for a rock of offence (Isa. viii:14). Two facts are mentioned by Him. Those who fall against Him, who oppose Him, shall be broken, and those upon whom the stone falls shall be ground to powder. The Jews fell against this stone when He was on earth and as a result they were broken as a nation. But the same stone which became the rejected stone is to crush down, strike, and grind to powder. There can be no question but He refers to the smiting stone in Nebuchadnezzar's dream image, that He is the stone and when He falls from above, it means His second coming, when Gentile political rule over the nations ends forever and when, "The God of heaven shall set up a kingdom, which shall never be destroyed, and the kingdom shall not be left to other people, but it shall break in pieces and consume all these kingdoms, and it shall stand forever" (Dan. ii:44). But what did our Lord mean when He said that the kingdom should be given to another nation? Some say He meant the Church, but nowhere is the Church

called a nation. Now the kingdom which will fill the whole
earth is not only the Lord's, but it is also Israel's kingdom.
It was a very intelligent question which the disciples asked
of their departing Lord: "Wilt Thou at this time restore the
Kingdom to Israel?" (Acts i:9). We know His answer. He
did not deny there would be a restoration of the Kingdom
to Israel, for all His holy prophets speak of such a restoration. The nation which will receive the Kingdom when the
times of the Gentiles end, is that part of Israel which has
turned to the Lord, the remnant of Israel. That remnant,
symbolized in the Book of Revelation as the 144,000 (Chapter vii) will inherit the Kingdom and then bring the fruit
thereof.

The *seventh chapter of Daniel* covers in its first part the
times of the Gentiles, the same as Nebuchadnezzar's dream
image does, only the four world empires are here seen as
ferocious beasts. All nations maintain their beastly character until their dominion ends (Dan. vii). The fourth great
beast, a mighty nondescript, awe-inspiring and terrifying
with the prominent little horn, a vicious dictator, represents
the revived Roman Empire in its final aspect domineering
over, and controlling all Europe. Then the scene changes.
Something happens from above, just as something happened
from above when the stone cut out without hands demol-
ished the entire man-image.

We listen once more to Daniel and quote again the
fundamental passage. "I saw in the night visions, and, behold,
one like the Son of Man came with the clouds of heaven, and
came to the Ancient of Days, and they brought Him near
before Him. And there was given Him dominion, and
glory, and a kingdom, that all people, nations and languages
should serve Him. His dominion is an everlasting dominion,
which shall not pass away, and His Kingdom which shall
not be destroyed" (Dan. vii:13, 14).

For the true believer all this is extremely plain. He knows
who this Son of Man is. Not so the rationalistic expositor,
if he deserves that name. He labors hard to disprove
what the Church has always believed. The modern critic

tells us, as we learn from "The Century Bible," that the
Son of Man is not an individual at all. It has nothing
whatever to do with Christ. It is not Messianic Prophecy.
They tell us the Son of Man is the symbolic representative
of supernatural beings, viz., of the saintly Israel transformed.
Such a theory is far fetched and distressingly unscholarly
and nonsensical. Everything in this vision calls for a
Person, a divine Person, and not a set of people. This view
is all out of harmony with the verse which follows after the
mention of the Son of Man. "All peoples, nations and
languages" are to "serve *Him*." Now to take the singular
"*Him*" in a figurative collective sense when put in such
close contrast with nouns such as "peoples," "nations and
languages," is not only incorrect but illogical and unreasonable. But the whole thing is contradictory. A "figurative
meaning" is assigned to "Him" and a literal meaning to
"peoples, nations and languages." But this is not the
worst done with this sublime prophecy. Others have
made the ridiculous statement that the whole vision of
Daniel confirms the process of evolution. Gradually the
beastly in man, the lion, the bear and the leopard character
disappears, and culture, art and science are represented by
the Son of Man! At such statements one is forced to laugh,
and then to weep over such deplorable blindness.

Has our Lord anything to say about this sublime vision?
Does He confirm and interpret it? We turn to one of the
most impressive scenes in His earthly life. The first thing
they did to Him, the willing victim, after His arrest in the
garden, was to lead Him to the high priest's palace, where the
Sanhedrin was assembled. Then the false, malicious, lying
witnesses arose. What majestic glory even then shone forth
through His behavior. He answered not a word! He held
His peace! The high priest, corrupt Caiaphas, became
impatient. When the Lord's silence continued he said unto
Him, "I adjure thee by the living God, that thou tell us
whether thou be the Christ, the Son of God." He could not
remain silent at such a question. Silence then would have
been wrong. He broke His silence.

"Jesus saith unto him, Thou hast said; nevertheless I say unto you, Hereafter ye shall see the Son of Man sitting on the right hand of power, and coming in the clouds of heaven" (Matt. xxvi:57-63). What does this answer mean? First of all He witnessed to His Deity, that He is the Son of God. Then He speaks of Himself as the Son of Man and quotes the one hundred and tenth psalm. As David's Son and David's Lord He is to sit at the right hand of power, that is at God's right hand. In the third place He assures the high priest that as Son of Man He is coming some day in the clouds of heaven. In the latter statement He confirmed and interpreted Daniel's vision and assures the high priest that He Himself is that Son of Man. The same confirmation was uttered by Him before, when He said: "They shall see the Son of Man coming in the clouds of heaven with power and great glory" (Matt. xxiv:30). The high priest rent his garment and pronounced Him a blasphemer worthy of death. But there is an interesting side light to the action of Caiaphas.

About one hundred years before Christ, part of a book was written which later appeared under the title "The Book of Enoch." In this spurious writing is a section known as the Similitudes. These reflect the belief of Jewish commentators, a hundred or more years before the birth of our Lord, as to the Deity, the character and attributes of the Messiah, especially His coming to be Judge and King. Now, these Similitudes speak of Daniel vii:13, 14 as Messianic. The question "Who is this Son of Man?" is answered as follows: "This is the Son of Man who hath righteousness, with whom dwelleth righteousness, and who revealeth all the treasures of that which is hidden, because the Lord of Spirits hath chosen Him, and whose lot hath the pre-eminence before the Lord of Spirits for ever." Then we read of His pre-existence "before the sun and the signs were created, before the stars of heaven were made" Furthermore, that Son of Man, according to these Similitudes, is "to sit on the throne of glory." "His glory is for ever and ever, and His might unto all generations. He puts down the mighty from their thrones.

He is to be the light of the Gentiles, and all shall serve the dominion of His Anointed that He may be potent and mighty on the earth." We repeat, though the book of Enoch is not an inspired book, yet it reflects the Messianic beliefs of the Jews and the Messianic interpretation of the passage in Daniel.*

Now Caiaphas and the gathered Sanhedrin, all scholars deeply versed in the literature of their nation, students of the apocalyptic writings produced during the previous two centuries, knew that the Son of Man coming in the clouds of heaven must be the Messiah, a Divine Being, the Immanuel. Hence Caiaphas, answering the claims of our Lord, addressed the Sanhedrin. All understood that the prisoner before them had said in unmistakeable words that He is the Son of Man, whom Daniel had seen five hundred years before in the night vision, whom their own apocalyptic writers had declared to be a supernatural Person, destined to rule and reign over all nations. Whom then shall we believe? The Lord Jesus Christ who facing the sure condemnation of His enemies, witnessing to the facts of His Deity, His enthronement at the right hand of God, and His return in the clouds of heaven, or the puerile inventions of finite creatures, who in pride of intellect claim a scholarship which is superior to Him who is the omniscient Lord? Any thinking Christian knows the right answer.

But in view of the vision of Daniel about the Son of Man coming in the clouds of heaven, and our Lord's remarkable confirmation of that vision and application to Himself, what becomes of the theory, so widely accepted in Christendom, that the Messianic Kingdom started on Pentecost, that it has been in the world ever since, that it is still growing, subduing nations and making rapidly for world conquest? We write in the summer of 1938. There is an unprecedented world chaos. This is true politically and economically. The whole world is heading for a tremendous bankruptcy.

---

*"As It Was—So Shall It Be." One of this series gives valuable information on the Book of Enoch.

No pact of European powers can arrest it; nor will the
unbalanced wild schemes of a "New Deal" with its outrageous
spending program save the United States from an impending
future crash. In religious matters the long predicted
apostasy gains in power. As stated before, Atheism and
Antichristianity are on the increase. Their field is no
longer the world which lieth in the wicked one, they are
prospering in Christendom. *Where is that Messianic
Kingdom?*

No Kingdom till the King comes back; no return of the
King till the predicted events of the very end of our age
are here; no end of the age with its satanic manifestations,
till the true Church has been called home.

And the preceding events, during the end of our age,
events which must come to pass before the Son of Man
appears from heaven in His kingly majesty, are likewise
revealed in the Book of Daniel. Our Lord confirms all in
His prophetic Olivet discourse. He called attention especially to the *abomination of desolation* which is not the Papacy,
but the abomination of the final Antichrist (Matt. xxiv:15).
He speaks of the faithful witnesses who will preach the
Gospel of the Kingdom also mentioned by Daniel (Dan.
xii:3; Matt. xxiv:14). He tells us that the age will end
with, "a great tribulation, such as was not since the beginning of the world to this time, no, nor ever shall be"; He
put His seal to Daniel's prophecy (Dan. xii:1; Matt. xxiv:
21). There is the misleading theory, adopted in Christendom, that the announced great tribulation is a thing of the
past and no future universal tribulation needs to be expected
since it came in 70 A. D. when Jerusalem was destroyed.
The words of our Lord explode this interpretation. The
one word used by Him shows that the tribulation is still
future. It is the word *immediately*. "Immediately after
the tribulation of those days shall the sun be darkened, and
the moon shall not give her light, and the stars shall fall
from heaven, and the powers of the heavens shall be shaken.
And then shall appear the sign of the Son of Man in heaven;
and then shall all the tribes of the earth mourn, and *they*

shall see the Son of Man coming in the clouds of heaven with power and great glory." Did all this happen *immediately* after the destruction of Jerusalem? No! Daniel's time of great trouble, confirmed by our Lord's prediction of "the great tribulation," is still future, not far away, for all is ready for such a time; the shadows of it are lengthening.

Now when our Lord spoke of Himself as coming in the clouds of heaven with power and great glory, He certainly meant a *literal*, a personal, a glorious as well as a visible coming. He announced this future coming a number of times. In the Gospel of Luke His words tell us clearly, that when He returns He will not find a converted world, a peaceful world, a world of righteousness. We quote His words: "And there shall be signs in the sun, and in the moon, and in the stars; and *upon earth distress of nations, with perplexity*; the sea and the waves roaring, men's hearts failing them for fear, and for looking after those things which are coming on the earth; for the powers of heaven shall be shaken. And they shall see the Son of Man coming in a cloud with power and great glory" (Luke xxi:25-27).

Who dares to say that He did not mean what He said? Who dares to meddle with this solemn promise of a personal return and explain it as meaning a spiritual coming at different periods of history. We give a sample of it from a volume which deals with Advent Certainties.

"Yes, He has been coming indeed, and the story of His Church is the record of His return. He has come in every crisis when under pressure of adversity the Christian community has been thrown back upon the ultimate sources whence she draws her strength—not upon wealth, nor inherited influence, nor the power of her apologetic; not her numbers, nor her machinery, but upon Him who is her life. Christ came back when amid the growing materialism of the Papacy the little poor man of Assissi gained a vision of what it meant to bear the cross after Jesus, and after his own fashion translated that vision into life. Christ came back when Luther, His warrior monk, forged his brave way through the barricades of medieval superstition to the heart of the Gospel of pardon and acceptance in the justifying grace of God. Christ came back when the Wesleys and those who had heard the Evangel through their teaching told anew the eighteenth century England the story of the cross. Christ came back in days nearer our own when men who were moved by His holy love and pity struck hard at the slave trade and the abuses of labor in factories and mines, and called upon the conscience of their country to recognize its duty to the negro, the prisoner and the child-worker. . . . Christ is coming back into our midst today in the sense of brotherhood which recognizes the call, not of a mere political party, but of the Son of Man Himself, to sweep away our social evils. Where His Church is, Christ is coming. Wherever He invades and touches human life, there He is coming back. These are the signs of His coming Kingdom! These are the prints of His Advent feet."*

We do not call this interpretation but *evaporation*. Others tell us when He promised to come again and to receive His own unto Himself, means death. The late Presbyterian Professor, Dr. Snowden, declared that the promised first resurrection (so vitally linked in Scripture with Christ's personal return) passed into history when during the world war the spirit of Washington and Lincoln was resurrected and found a re-incarnation in the soldiers of the battlefield. And today some deluded religious leaders acclaim even radical movements as fulfilling Bible prophecy, in giving relief to the poor and peace to a war stricken world. It shows where men will drift to if they deny the plainest statements of the Scriptures in their literal meaning. Spiritualization and allegorization are like quicksand, the more one labors, the deeper one sinks.

But let us also remind ourselves of the Transfiguration recorded in the synoptic Gospels. On that holy mountain His face shone like the sun, and His raiment was white as light. The three disciples, who were with Him "saw His glory" (Luke ix:32). The Transfiguration was the fore-gleam of His glory. Such glory He received when God raised Him from among the dead. Such glory will be His on the day of His return, not a spiritual, but a visible glory. Peter, one of the eyewitnesses of the Transfiguration glory,

---

*"Advent Certainties."

speaks of it as making known "the power and coming of our Lord Jesus Christ" (2 Peter i:16). Then Peter in view of what he and his fellow disciples saw, wrote, "We have also a more sure word of prophecy." The more correct rendering is, "We have the word of prophecy made more sure." But is the word of Prophecy not sure already? How then can it be made more sure? The answer is quite simple, the Old Testament reveals a great, coming day, the day of the Lord. On that day heaven will open and the Lord of Glory will be manifested. This Lord of Glory is Christ. The Transfiguration scene has made the prophecy of the glorious manifestation on the day of the Lord more real and more sure. But how many other Scripture passages from the prophets we could cite, all confirmed by the testimony of our Lord. Isaiah xiii:9-13 gives a prophetic picture of the day of the Lord and our Lord quoted these words and applied them to His return. In the same chapter Isaiah wrote, "I will shake the heavens." Add to this the words of Haggai, "For thus saith the Lord of hosts, yet once, it is in a little while, and I will shake the heavens and the earth, and the sea, and the dry land, and I will shake all nations, and the desire of all nations shall come, and I will fill this house with glory, saith the Lord" (Hag. ii:6, 7). Our Lord said in connection with His future coming, "The powers of the heavens shall be shaken." Read also Isaiah xiv:23; Ezekiel xxxii:7; Hab. iii:3, 4,11. Joel, the great seer of the day of the Lord, what precedes and what follows, wrote likewise of the same events, alluded to by our Lord as meaning Himself. "The sun and the moon shall be darkened, and the stars shall withdraw their shining. The Lord also shall roar out of Zion, and utter His voice from Jerusalem; and the heavens and the earth shall be shaken, but the Lord will be the hope of His people, and the strength of the children of Israel" (Joel iii:15, 16).

Inasmuch as we find so much in Old Testament prophecy about the re-gathering of Israel and the future glory of Jerusalem we must quote our Lord in His confirmation of these prophecies. We quote three statements.

In Luke's Gospel He announced the fate of the Jews and of Jerusalem, after both had rejected Him. "And they shall fall by the edge of the sword, and shall be led away captive into all nations, and Jerusalem shall be trodden down of the Gentiles, until the times of the Gentiles are fulfilled" (Luke xxi:24). This is the only place in Scripture in which the times of the Gentiles are mentioned. They began with Nebuchadnezzar, king of Babylon. Since then Jerusalem has been under the heel of Gentile dominion. Their world-wide dispersion began after the Roman armies had destroyed the city and burned the temple in the year 70. Our Lord with loud lamentation had announced the terrible fate of the city forty years before. All came literally to pass (Luke xix:41-44). But is this world-wide dispersion of the nation final? Jerusalem is still in the hands of Gentiles, for the British who have the mandate are not Israelites, but Gentiles. Is this to continue for ever? Is there no change coming? If so it would surely mean that the many Old Testament prophecies concerning a future earthly Jerusalem, from which the world government of righteousness and peace will proceed, should either be spiritualized, or else branded as wild dreams of Jewish patriots. There is still a chapter of Jerusalem's history unwritten. The hordes of Gog and Magog are yet to gather before the gates of the modern, restored Jerusalem. The Northern army Joel beheld in the ninth century B. C. is still to come and likewise the remarkable deliverance of the city as described by Zechariah (Zech. xiv).

Our Lord confirms all these facts, promises and prophecies, which belong exclusively to the earthly Jerusalem, by the one sentence "until the times of the Gentiles are fulfilled." These words, beyond the shadow of a doubt, tell us there is coming a great change for Jerusalem. That change comes when the allotted times of the Gentiles have expired. When that day comes with the visible manifestation of the Lord, our Lord and Israel's Messiah, it will bring the literal fulfilment of Jerusalem's restoration and glorification.

In order to prevent confusion we mention another term used by Paul in his great prophetic testimony concerning Israel in the eleventh chapter of Romans. He revealed a mystery when he wrote with his Spirit-guided pen, "Blindness in part is happened to Israel, until the fulness of the Gentiles be come in" (Rom. xi:25).

"The fulness of the Gentiles" does not mean, as it has been paraphrased in a New Testament in twentieth century English, "till the rest of the world is converted." It does not mean that at all; it means, till the full number of the out-called Gentiles, constituting the true Church, has been reached. It is not synonymous with the fulfilment of the times of the Gentiles. When the fulness of the Gentiles comes in, the Church, the body of Christ, being joined to the Lord, the head of the body, as revealed in First Thessalonians iv:16-18, the times of the Gentiles are still in power. In fact, the real ending of the times of the Gentiles cannot come, until the fulness of the Gentiles has come in, and God's purpose in this age, the calling out from all nations of a people for His name, is accomplished.

We now turn to another brief statement of our Lord, which confirms Israel's promised future redemption. At the close of that remarkable chapter in Matthew, in which He denounced the religious leaders of His day, scribes and Pharisees, as hypocrites, blind guides, fools, serpents and generation of vipers, He sounded a great note of hope. "Behold, your house is left unto you desolate. For I say unto you, Ye shall not see Me henceforth, *till ye shall say, Blessed is He that cometh in the name of the Lord*" (Matt. xxiii:38, 39). What does it mean? (1) Their house would be left desolate. He had come to His own and they received Him not. He would leave them and henceforth they would not see Him. We are reminded of Hosea v:15: "I will return to my place, till they acknowledge their offence, in their affliction they will seek Me early." (2) But He also holds out hope for them, they will see Him again. It has a condition, "till ye shall say, Blessed is He that cometh in the name of the Lord." This is a quotation from the one hun-

dred and eighteenth Psalm (verse 26). The context contains the prophecy of the rejected stone, which has become
the head of the corner (verse 22). Here is mentioned "the
day" the Lord has made, that is, the day of His appearing
(verse 24). In that day He will receive a welcome and an
acknowledgment from those who had rejected Him. But
in order to acknowledge Him, a part of the nation must have
believed on Him *before* His return. Else how could they
say, "Blessed is He that cometh in the name of the Lord"?
Certainly not the atheistic, the radical and corrupt part of
the Jews, who are opposed to Him, who side with the coming man of sin, the Antichrist, the false Messiah. When
that masterpiece of Satan appears and takes his place in the
yet to be built temple in Jerusalem, these apostates will
worship him and receive the mark of the beast. For such
judgment is in store. They cannot escape because they are
Jews, as some teach. They will be cut off from the land.
But a part of the nation had a remarkable experience. As
already quoted, blindness in part has happened to Israel
until the fulness of the Gentiles comes in. When the
the fulness of the Gentiles, their number completed and the
testimony of the true Church ceases on earth, the veil will
be taken away from a portion of the people Israel. These
according to the testimony of the prophets and the Psalms
will witness for the coming King and will suffer. It is this
believing remnant which will say, "Blessed is He that cometh
in the name of the Lord." They will receive the kingdom
and then all the unfulfilled promises to national Israel will
be realized.

We have still another prophecy of our Lord to consider
which is perhaps the most important. We turn again to the
Olivet Discourse. The first thing our Lord mentions which
will take place after His return is the following: "And He
shall send His angels with a great sound of a trumpet, and
they shall gather together His elect from the four winds,
from one end of heaven to the other" (Matt. xxv:31). Some
expositors teach that this gathering of the elect is the gathering of the Church. But that is impossible. The Church is

gathered before the visible coming of the Lord; the Church will meet Him first of all, not on earth, but in the heavenlies. Then the Church comes back with the Lord in glory in fulfilment of such New Testament Scriptures as 1 Thessalonians iii13; 2 Thessalonians i:10; Revelation xix:14 and others. Furthermore the home-gathering of the Church is not done by angels, but as predicted in 1 Thessalonians iv:16-18, by the shout of the Lord, the voice of the archangel and the trump of God. When the call comes for the Church to meet her Lord in the air, those who died in Christ will be raised. But resurrection is not mentioned at all by our Lord in His prophetic discourse. And finally this gathering from the four winds cannot be the Church for the elect in the synoptic Gospels do not mean the Church. It means Israel each time it is used in the Gospels. This fact is much strengthened by another, the Lord mentions the fig tree next, an emblem also of Israel. Postmillennialists and the new-comer into the family of objectors to Premillennialism, the Amillennialists, deny that there ever will be a regathering of Israel and an earthly kingdom in which Israel will be the head. Our Lord in the quoted words confirms the literalness of the many prophecies which deal with a restoration of all the tribes of Israel to their God-given land. We quoted a number of these promises of national restoration in the previous chapter (see also Isa. xxvii:13).

The final part of the Olivet Discourse (Matt. xxv:31-46) is not a parable, but a description of a judgment which will be executed by the Lord after His return. It has been misnamed "the universal judgment of the last day." The Bible does not teach a universal judgment, nor a universal resurrection. There are two resurrections, the first and the second, but between them is a time-period fixed by the Word of God. The judgment of which our Lord speaks in His discourse is a judgment of *living* nations. He says nothing whatever about the dead. Nations are judged. Some disappear forever; others enter into the kingdom. This is not a heavenly kingdom, but the kingdom "prepared from the foundation of the world," as planned by God in His purposes of redemption.   We are not writing an exposition of this future judgment of nations.*   Our Lord confirms Joel iii:1-2, as well as other prophecies which reveal Him as the future Judge of all nations.

We have heard it said that Christ had nothing to say in His teachings about a future reign of Himself.   This has been claimed as an evidence that His second coming will bring the end of all things, generally called "the end of the world."   The passages in the Old Testament, in which such reign is promised, it is said, mean a spiritual reign.   As to a thousand year reign, promised in the Apocalypse, that is put down as having too slender a support in Scripture to be accepted.   We disagree with these conclusions.

Twice our Lord speaks of "the throne of His glory."   At once we are told that He is upon the throne of His glory *now*, therefore when He spoke of the throne of His glory, He meant His exaltation to the right hand of God.   This view is unscriptural.   He Himself gives us the conclusive evidence that there is a difference between the Father's throne, where He sits at the right hand of the majesty on high, and His own throne.   We listened to the final promise made in His church-messages in the Apocalypse.   "To him that over-cometh will I grant to sit with Me in *my throne*; even as I also overcame, and am set down with My Father in *His* throne" (Rev. iii:21).   Who can claim in the presence of this statement that His own throne is the Father's throne? That throne was mentioned by Gabriel's message to the Virgin of Nazareth, "The Lord God shall give unto Him the throne of His father David."   He did not receive that throne when He went back to heaven, for David's throne is not in heaven but on earth.   And the throne which belongs to Him, the throne He is worthy of, is given to Him by His Father, not now, but at the time of His return to earth.   There is a hymn which Christians often thoughtlessly sing.   A stanza reads:

---

*See the author's "Olivet Discourse."

"King of kings in heaven we'll crown Him
When our journey is complete."

Think of the Church crowning Him King in heaven! The crowning will not take place in heaven but on earth. But where is it written that it needs His second coming to receive His own throne? "When the Son of man shall come in His glory, and all the holy angels with Him, *then* shall He sit upon the throne of His glory" (Matt. xxv:31). God does the crowning; God enthrones Him in the holy hill of Zion; God puts all things under His feet; God gives to Him the reign of glory from sea to sea, unto the uttermost parts of the earth. But will that throne really exist a thousand years, as announced six times in the final book of the Bible? This also is answered by the Word of God. When He returns, according to the one hundred and tenth Psalm, He is to rule in the midst of His enemies, not over a converted world. His reign will begin with the subjugation of all His enemies. "For He must reign, till He has put all enemies under His feet" (1 Cor. xv:25).

Let us look at the second passage in which He speaks of His throne. It is found in the nineteenth chapter of Matthew. The rich young man had gone away from Him sorrowful. After the words spoken by our Lord, Peter's voice is heard. "Peter said unto Him, Behold, we have forsaken all, and followed Thee; what shall we have therefore?" In other words, what will be our gain, our reward, our glory, because we have been faithful?

Did He tell them of earthly gains, earthly possessions, earthly glory, during the present age? He speaks of the future, a definite future. "And Jesus said unto them, Verily I say unto you, that ye which have followed Me; in the regeneration when the Son of man shall sit in the throne of His glory, ye also shall sit upon twelve thrones, judging the twelve tribes of Israel" (Matt. xix:23-30). This is a promise of reward. The reward will not be given till He has His own throne. We can think here of Paul's teachings as to rewards and his final words from the Roman prison. "I have fought a good fight, I have finished my course. I have kept the

faith. Henceforth there is laid up for me a crown of righteousness, which the Lord, the righteous Judge, shall give me
at *that day*; and not to me only, but unto all them also that
love His appearing" (2 Tim. iv:7-8). Such was Paul's hope,
and such is ours also.

We must now call attention to a single word, used by our
Lord; it is the word "regeneration." He speaks of the
regeneration and connects it with His throne. When this
regeneration comes He will be upon His throne. There can
be no regeneration till He occupies that throne.

Every Christian knows what this word means individ-
ually. It means to experience a new birth by believing on
the Son of God, the Lord Jesus who died for our sins. "Not
by works of righteousness which we have done, but according to His mercy He saved us, by the bath of regeneration,
and renewing of the Holy Spirit" (Titus iii:5). "Therefore
if any man be in Christ, he is a new creation; old things are
passed away; behold, all things are become new" (2 Cor.
v:17). This is all the world has seen up to the present time,
the regeneration of individuals, the power of the Gospel of
Jesus Christ manifested in all who believe. But here the
word is used in a wider and greater sense. There is coming
a regeneration which will be experienced by Israel, by
nations, and also by creation itself. "Behold, I make all
things new" (Rev. xxi:5), that blessed and glorious goal of
redemption. These assuring words of hope, spoken by Himself, will some day be fully accomplished. This is the meaning of the word "regeneration" employed by our Lord in
His answer to Peter. It cannot come through human
agencies, nor through scientific discoveries, inventions, no,
not even through the Church or great spiritual revivals,
outranging all former activities of the Holy Spirit. The
Son of man must return, receive the throne of His glory
and then follows the regeneration. It will be the result of
His work on the cross and bring the display of His redemption power. The best commentary on the word "regeneration," as used by our Lord, is given by the Spirit of God in
the third chapter of the Book of Acts. The mouthpiece is

Peter in giving his second testimony to the Jews in Jerusalem.
An evidence has been furnished that the One whom they
crucified is alive and is at the right hand of God. The
miracle of healing of the lame man at the temple gate called
"Beautiful" demonstrated all this. Then Peter gave them
the truth once more. "Ye denied the Holy One and the
Just, and desired a murderer to be given unto you; and
killed the Prince of Life, whom God hath raised from the
dead; whereof we are witnesses." After that comes the great
testimony which defines the coming regeneration.

"Repent ye therefore, that your sins may be blotted out,
when the times of refreshing shall come from the presence
of the Lord; and He shall send Jesus Christ, who before was
preached unto you, whom the heavens must receive until
the times of restoration of all things, which God hath spoken
by the mouth of all His holy prophets since the world began"
(Acts iii:19-21). On the day of Pentecost Peter had quoted,
under the guidance of the Spirit, the one hundred and tenth
Psalm and applied it to the crucified One, that He ascended
into heaven, and took His place at the right hand of God.
This truth he states once more, the heavens received Him.
But is He going to remain there forever? Peter tells us
that God will send His Son again, the same who had been
preached unto them. He employs that little word of hope
"until." The Lord Jesus Christ has been received by the
heavens "until the times of restitution of all things." Mighty
truths these are! His physical resurrection; His physical
acension; His physical presence in heaven at the right hand
of God and His physical return. His return will bring the
restoration of all things.

The restoration of all things is the regeneration which
follows the return of our Lord and His enthronement. It
brings the times of refreshing. There is still another great
fact mentioned which we must not pass by. The restoration of all things is not left to be defined by our imagination,
but it is the restoration, "spoken by the mouth of all His
holy prophets since the world began." What restoration,
have God's holy prophets predicted? All that we have

stated before. The restoration of Israel, their regeneration
as well; the restoration of the theocracy, the tabernacle of
David (Acts xv:16); the establishment of the kingdom; the
conversion of Gentile nations, joined unto the Lord and all
other predictions of hope including the removal of the curse
which rests upon creation, peace on earth and glory to God
in the Highest. Such will be the regeneration, when the
Son of man sits upon the throne of His glory. There is a
teaching which gains ground, even among some teachers of
prophecy, that the restitution or restoration of all things
includes the wicked dead. But the prophets do not teach
"the restitution" of the wicked, the lost. It is an invention.

We have seen from the testimony of our Lord that He
confirms the testimony of the prophets and that His interpretation is a literal one. We have seen the great hope which
will bring the realization of all promised blessings is His
second coming. Apart from His return there is no hope.
Distinctively different is the hope of the Church, which is
nowhere mentioned in the prophetic testimony of our Lord
in the synoptic Gospels. He gives the initial notes of "that
blessed Hope" in the Gospel of John (xi:25, xiv:1-3, xvii:24)
its full revelation, His coming for His saints to meet Him
in the air, for a glorious entrance into the Father's house
with its many mansions, is given by the Holy Spirit in the
Epistles; it is one of the great doctrines of our Christian
faith.

Our next chapters will trace the hope historically from
apostolic times down to our own times. We will show that
true, scriptural Premillennialism, that Christ comes again
to fulfil the promises made unto the fathers, to enact the
second part of the Protevangel of Eden (Gen. iii:15), the
glorious flowering of it, when the prince of this world, the
god of this age will be dethroned and God's King of glory
will be enthroned, has been the faith of the true Church
from apostolic days, and in these latter times has been
restored to the Church in its scriptural, pristine meaning. It
has been sadly distorted and perverted in the past, and also
in our own days, through the power of Satan. World con-

ditions today are the strongest evidences, that Premillennialism is true and all other theories, such as Postmillennialism and Amillennialism, can no longer be maintained.

PART II

THE HOPE IN HISTORY

FROM APOSTOLIC DAYS TO OUR TIMES

THE APPROACHING REALIZATION

CHAPTER I

The Testimony of the Apostles and the Apostolic Fathers

In the preceding chapters we have shown from Scripture the mass of prophecies relating to the oath bound covenant promises of Israel, to the Gentile nations and the world-wide kingdom, into which the nations of the earth will be gathered to be governed by the King of Righteousness and Peace, the King of kings and the Lord of lords. We have also learned that the curse which rests upon creation must some day be removed for such is creation's hope. All these promises have a *literal* meaning. The literal is the final goal of prophecy. Corporicity is the end of the ways of God.

Up to the present time, approaching the middle of the twentieth century, the world knows nothing of the fulfilment of these prophecies. There is not even that strained and much used "spiritual fulfilment," which in reality is non-existent. Furthermore we have shown in a scriptural and logical way that there can be no fulfilment of any of these promises of hope and glory during the course of our age, which "lieth in the wicked one" (1 John v:19). It is governed by the prince of this age, who is its god. The dethronement of Satan, the old serpent, the dragon that is the devil, the crushing of his head, can be accomplished by one Person only. That Person is He who suffered and died on the cross, who is risen from among the dead, exalted to the right hand, where He awaits the Father's time to return to earth, so abundantly revealed in both Testaments. Hence the fulfilment of every hope, the Church's hope, Israel's hope, the nations' hope, creation's hope, is entirely dependent on that future great event, His visible and glorious appearing.

We also have shown that our Lord in His prophetic testimony in the synoptic Gospels has confirmed, endorsed, and interpreted the leading prophecies of the Old Testament. He did not promise a spiritual coming, or a spiritual fulfilment of all the prophets have spoken, but a literal one.

An interesting task is now before us. We want to trace this hope in history, beginning with the apostolic age, through the early centuries, the Middle Ages, the Reformation period, through more recent times down to the year 1938 A.D. We want to see and learn from history that the Church in the beginning held this hope, how it was perverted and degraded, became the victim of fanaticism, carnality, immoralities, and all kinds of heresies. We want to show when and how it was abandoned, what subtle and strange inventions were substituted for it. We shall trace its revival, how in a pre-Reformation period, interest in prophecy was awakened, what the reformers believed, and how gradually the forgotten hope was restored till in the beginning of the nineteenth century the Holy Spirit through chosen instruments gave back to the Church "that blessed hope" in its scriptural meaning.

I. *The Hope of the Coming of the Lord as Revealed in the New Testament Epistles*. The first Church history is contained in the Book of Acts, covering about thirty years. We have already pointed out the striking testimony of Peter as to the return of the Lord and the blessed results which will follow that event. There is another equally comprehensive and enlightening statement which shows the Apostolic faith and hope. They had gathered for the first General Assembly in Jerusalem to decide the status of Gentile converts (Acts xv:1-12). During this gathering, James, the representative of the Jewish-Christian Church in Jerusalem spoke the following words: "Men and Brethren, hearken unto me. Simeon hath declared how God at the first did visit the Gentiles, to take out of them a people for His name. And to this agree the words of the prophets; as it is written, after this I will return, and will build again the tabernacle of David, which is fallen down; and I will build again the ruins thereof, and I will set it up, that the residue of men might seek after the Lord, and all the Gentiles, upon whom My name is called, saith the Lord who doeth all these things" (Acts xv:13-17). There was no dissenting voice among the gathered delegates. They were all what we term Premillennialists. They believed in the great work of the age, the gathering of a people for His name (the Church); when that is completed and the fulness of the Gentiles comes in, Christ will return; His return will mean the establishment of the tabernacle of David, the promised kingdom with David's throne; and after that the turning of the Gentiles to the Lord. They were Jews who had accepted Christ as their promised Messiah. They knew their own Scriptures. They knew that their national promises, their restoration, and the promised kingdom would come when He, whom many of them had seen after His resurrection, whom the Apostles had seen ascending into heaven, comes again.

Only in a brief way can we trace in the New Testament epistles this hope, as taught by the Holy Spirit, but we shall say enough to prove that the hope of the coming of the Lord is one of the vital doctrines of our Christian faith. Take it out of these great documents, paraphrase or ignore it, and the Gospel itself becomes a mutilated Gospel and salvation would lead nowhere. In fact, the most important doctrines of Christianity cannot be maintained inasmuch as they rest upon that hope, the hope which is the golden thread woven into our supernatural Christianity. The three essentials of Christianity are tersely given by Paul in the epistle to Titus (ii:11-15). Salvation first, this is followed by a life lived soberly, righteously, and godly. Many stop here. But there is something else. "Looking for that blessed hope, and the glorious appearing of the great God and our Saviour Jesus Christ." Such was Apostolic teaching and preaching.

It was only fitting that the man of God, Paul, who had received that mystery from the Lord, which was not made known in former ages (Ephes. iii:1-10), should also make known by direct revelation that hope, which is specifically the hope of the body and bride of Christ, that is the Church. The first epistle Paul wrote is the one addressed to the Church in Thessalonica. At the close of the first chapter we find the same three great essentials (verses 9 and 10). The third is, "to wait for His Son from heaven, even Jesus, who delivereth us from the wrath to come." In the same epistle he makes known what he had received "by the Word of the Lord," that unique revelation which has been the comfort and cheer of uncountable thousands (iv:16-18). "For the Lord Himself shall descend from heaven with a shout, with the voice of the archangel, and with the trump of God; and the dead in Christ shall rise first; then we which are alive and remain shall be caught up together with them in clouds; to meet the Lord in the air; and so shall we ever be with the Lord." This is indeed a *new* revelation. No such hope is mentioned by the prophets. Here is not the Son of man coming in a cloud back to earth again, but the righteous dead, with those alive at that time, are taken up in the clouds to meet, not Himself as Son of man, but as Lord in the air. Resurrection and transformation are here definitely promised, besides a blessed re-union of all the saints of God —"together with them." Nothing is said in this revelation about a preceding "great tribulation"; not a word is given on Antichrist, nor of a restored Roman empire nor any other signs, for the simple reason that these things come to pass after this blessed hope has been realized.

In some of Paul's epistles the distinction is also made between "the day of Christ" and "the day of the Lord." This is brought out in this first epistle. The gathering together of the saints brings the day of Christ, when He receives them in the Father's house; the day of the Lord is "that day" so prominent throughout the prophetic Word, is mentioned in the last chapter of first Thessalonians. We must not overlook the fact that even then the enemy of the Truth began to meddle with this blessed hope. This we learn from the Second Epistle to the Thessalonians (ii). From the same Epistle we learn another interesting fact. Though the Thessalonians were but a short time converted to Christ, yet Paul in ministering to them had taught them prophecy, the coming of the Lord and events connected with it (2 Thess. ii:5). In Romans the great hope is found in the eighth chapter (verses 15-30). In the same Epistle Israel's hope is

prominent.   Triumphantly Paul writes, "God hath not cast
away His people" (Israel).   There is coming for them a time
of fulness (Rom. xi:12); they are going to be received, which
will be life from the dead (verse 15); they are the broken
off branches now, while Gentiles are ingrafted branches; the
broken off branches will be put back upon their own good,
and that will be when the Lord deals in judgment with
Gentile, apostate Christendom (verses 16-24); all Israel
shall be saved (verse 26).   But all is dependent on His return.
In the Corinthian Epistles the Judgment seat of Christ is
made prominent before which believers will appear not to
decide salvation, but that works and service might be manifested.   Saints shall judge the world and angels (1 Cor.
vi:2, 3).   The great resurrection (chap. xv) states the coming
events and Christ's future reign on and over the earth
(xv:23-28) and gives once more the truth of 1 Thessalonians
iv:16-18.   (Verses 52-54) Second Corinthians has a great
chapter of hope. (chap. v).

Ephesians makes known the riches of grace, reveals the
dispensation of the fulness of times (i:10) and the inheritance
in store for the Church.   The passage of hope in Philippians
promises "a body fashioned like unto His glorious body"
(iii:20-21), but that will not be till He comes.   Colossians
announces that when Christ appears believers also shall
appear with Him in glory (iii:1-4).   The two Epistles to
Timothy contain the testimony as to the religious and moral
conditions before the Lord comes(1 Tim. iv; 2 Tim. iii; iv:1-4).
Hebrews witnesses to the same facts.   The Firstbegotten
will be brought into the inhabited earth (i:6); the inhabited
earth is not put in subjection of angels, but under the
feet of Him who was made a little lower than the angels
(ii:5-9); He is bringing many sons unto glory (ii:10); He
that was offered once to bear the sins of many will appear the
second time (ix:28); it is yet a little while and He that shall
come will come and will not tarry (x:37); we are to receive a
kingdom which cannot be moved (xii:28).   James bears his
testimony to the same truth (chap. v).   Peter testifies of
the future "revelation of Jesus Christ" and of the coming

of the Chief Shepherd who will give a crown of glory that fadeth not away (v:4). Nearly his entire second Epistle is taken up with His coming and the apostate conditions which precede it. The beloved disciple, John, exhorts the children of God to abide in Him, "that when He shall appear, we may have confidence, and not be ashamed before Him at His coming" (1 John iii:28). Precious are his Spirit given words of blessed assurance. "Beloved, now are we the children of God, and it doth not yet appear what we shall be; but we know that, when He shall appear, we shall be like Him; for we shall see Him as He is" (1 John iii:2).

Jude's Epistle gives an answer to those who think that the Church is going to save the world and establish His kingdom on earth. It reveals the worst apostasy of the end of our age. Then follows the capstone of the entire Revelation of God, the Apocalypse, with its great panorama of the end of our age, the judgments executed from above, the manifestation of the two beasts, out of the sea and out of the land, the mystical Babylon and its judgment and other future events. Majestically pictured is His Coming out of the opened heavens, accompanied by the redeemed; He comes to claim His title as King of kings and Lord of lords. Not till then shall heaven and earth hear the mighty shout of triumph and victory "the kingdoms of this world are become the kingdom of our Lord and His Christ; and He shall reign for ever and ever" (xi:15). Then the voices like mighty waters from above will be heard in their Hallelujah, vibrating through the vaults of the heavens, "Hallelujah, for the Lord God omnipotent reigneth" (xix:6). Then breaks the Day of the Lord with its judgment, its glory, bringing the fulfilment of all unfulfilled prophecies. The old serpent is put into the prison so that he can no longer deceive the nations. Six times it is stated that Christ will reign and His Saints with Him for a thousand years. Then righteousness and peace will be established, while His glory covers the earth as the waters cover the deep. Such is the unfolding of the hope of the ages and its glorious consummation in the New Testament. Such is the hope of His coming, not to end the *Kosmos*, the physical world, not to bring the end of all things, but to usher in an age, lasting a thousand years, which will demonstrate God's glorious victory through His Son, our Lord. Call it Premillennialism, Chiliasm, or by any other name, it is the truth and the only key which unlocks God's Word and makes clear the eternal purposes.

Over sixty-five years ago there was published a book which attempted to contradict this much maligned Premillennialism. The writer, Dr. David Brown, however made some fatal admissions, which became, with thinking people a strong argument for it. We quote:

"Premillennialists have done the Church a real service, by calling attention to the place which the Second Advent holds in the Word of God and the scheme of divine truth. If the controversy which they have raised should issue in a fresh and impartial inquiry into this branch of it, I, for one, instead of regretting, shall rejoice in the agitation of it. When they dilate upon the prominence given to this doctrine in Scripture, and the practical uses which are made of it, they touch a cord in the heart of every simple lover of his Lord, and carry conviction to all who tremble at His Word; so much so, that I am persuaded that nine-tenths of all who have embraced the Premillennial view of the Second Advent, have done so on the supposition that no other view of it will admit of an unfettered and unmodified use of the Scripture language on the subject—that it has its proper interpretation and full force only in this theory. . . . *With them we affirm that the Redeemer's second appearing is the very Polestar of the Church. That it is so held forth in the New Testament is beyond dispute.* Let anyone do himself the justice to collect and arrange the evidence on the subject, and he will be surprised—if the study be new to him— at once at the copiousness, the variety and the conclusiveness of it" (pages 12, 13).

"Nor is it in regard to the personal appearing of the Saviour only that Premillennialists will and ought to prevail against all who keep it out of sight. There is a *range of truth* connected with it which necessarily sinks out of its Scriptural position and influence whenever the coming of Christ is put out of its due place. I refer to the *resurrection* as a co-ordinate subject of the Church's hope, and to all the truths which circle around it, in which there is power to stir and to elevate, which nothing else, substituted for it, can ever

possess. The resurrection life of the Head as now animat-
ing all His members, and at length quickening them from
the tomb, to be forever with Him—these, and such like, are
truths in the presentation of which Premillennialists are cast
in the mould of Scripture, from which it is as vain, as it
were undesirable, to dislodge them" (Page 488).

And where do you find the men and women, who claim
to be Christians but who reject the authority of the written
Word of God, who sneer at the Virgin birth, who speak of
our Lord as a mere human being, who ridicule His self-
witness, who are the enemies of the cross of Christ, who
teach that resurrection is but a myth, who have dismissed
everything supernatural, yet maintain that they are Christians—where do you find them? Certainly not in the
company of those whose hope is a living Christ, a coming
Christ who comes to end what man cannot end, to bring
what man cannot bring, who believe all the prophets have
spoken and who earnestly wait for His Son from heaven.
Go to rationalistic modernism, there you will find them in
abundance. There are the scoffers who say, "Where is the
promise of His coming?" and the illogical assertion, based
upon the unproved evolution theory, "that since the fathers
fell asleep, all things continue as they were from beginning
of the creation" (2 Peter iii:1-7).

II. *The Apostolic Age and What Followed.* One of the
greatest scholars of Patristic literature of the early Church,
Dr. Adolf Harnack of Berlin, in his contribution to the
Encyclopaedia Britannica on the Millennium says: "Faith
in the nearness of Christ's second advent and the establishment of His reign of glory on the earth was undoubtedly a
strong point in the primitive Christian Church." He mentions the fact that this faith was widely prevalent amongst
the early Christians.

Let us imagine ourselves in the prosperous city of Ephesus
about the year 60. A.D. There was a splendid assembly, or
church, in existence, taught deeply and nourished well by
the Apostle Paul himself. Let us imagine it is Lord's day
morning, the first day of the week, which from the beginning

of the Church, had been set aside as the day of worship. It carried with it the hallowed memory of the resurrection of the Lord Jesus Christ from among the dead. And fifty days later the Paraclete, the Holy Spirit, on the same day had come from heaven to earth, to indwell believers, baptizing them at the same time into that body, the Church, of which Christ is the head. As we walked along one of the main streets of Ephesus, we should have seen the pagan inhabitants in their usual occupation and pleasure seeking crowds, men and women dressed in gaudy attire. But all at once we notice a group of people who outwardly differ from the heathen Ephesians. No flashy ornaments on women, no painted cheeks, no plaited hair; all reveals chastity and humility. They converse quietly in the vernacular of Asia Minor. Now several men and women join them and as they do they greet them with a greeting of strange sound. *Mara-natha!* Every mouth repeats the greeting. *Mara-natha!* The word is Aramaic and means, "Our Lord cometh." The Spirit of God had used it in a solemn statement given through Paul (1 Cor. xvi:22). Tradition tells us it was the daily greeting of Christians in the early Church. "Our Lord cometh!" It spurred them on to holy living, to follow Him, "Who when He was reviled, reviled not again; when He suffered, He threatened not; but committed it to Him that judgeth righteously" (1 Peter ii:23). Our Lord cometh! it brought them cheer in the midst of tribulation and persecution. "Our Lord cometh!" In a moment, in the twinkling of an eye! They did not lay up treasures on earth.

But let us follow this group of Christians on that Lord's day morning. They reach a simple dwelling. Here the Church meets for worship. We enter and find that all is simplicity. They gather as Christians, believers in the Lord Jesus Christ. They know nothing of the sad divisions of believers, which had their origin in the worldly assembly of Corinth (1 Cor. i:11-14). They have come, as it was the custom in Apostolic times, to express their loving obedience in carrying out His own request, "Do this in remembrance of Me." There stands the table with the loaf of bread and

alongside of it the cup filled with wine. What blessed simplicity prevails for a real spiritual worship, the worship in
Spirit and in Truth.

Before we proceed let us glance at one of the Eucharistic
celebrations of Roman Catholicism in our own times. What
pomp! Here are the presumed and assumed "Princes of the
Church!" What a riot of colors! They are arrayed in purple
and scarlet colors, decked with gold and precious stones and
pearls (Rev. xvii:4). What gorgeous music! What chant-
ings! Then comes the celebration; the invented transub-
stantiation, the sudden change of a piece of material bread,
the wafer, into the body of Christ. The wine becomes suddenly the very blood of Christ, shed afresh in this celebration of the Mass. The cup is withheld from the "laity."
The people fall down under the sound of sensual music to
"worship" supposedly. Eyes and ears have their feasts. It
is nothing new. Such perverted worship started in Babylon.
It is Babylonish (Dan. iii:1-7).

We return to that simple room in Ephesus in the year
60. A.D. They all chant a Psalm, or a hymn of praise.
Prayer follows, not a prayer in a set form read from a prayer
book, it is praise and prayer in the Spirit. That worthy
Name, the Name above every other name, is on all lips. In
vain do we wait to hear the name of the Virgin mother of
our Lord. Nor is there a presiding "clergyman." Someone
reads from a papyrus manuscript, perhaps a portion of the
Gospel or from some Epistle. All hearts are fixed on Him
who died on the Cross; they remember His suffering, His
deep soul agony and His shout of victory, "It is finished!"
Then all partake of the bread and the wine to show forth
His death; their hearts eat and drink of Him afresh in the
Spirit. *Till He come!* (1 Cor. xi:23-25). Maranatha! Our
Lord is coming! Joyfully hearts in holy anticipation look
forward to that promised face to face meeting. And as they
leave that simple place, after hearing a message from the
Word, the "till He come" lingers in their hearts and minds.

We follow a group of Christians again. They carry the
remains of a loved one to place the body in a resting place

in mother earth. Maranatha is heard once more. Tear
dimmed eyes look upward. Through their tears they
remember, "The Lord Himself shall come with a shout."
What the inspired pen of Paul had written is their blessed
hope. "Comfort ye one another with these words," is
done and tears are wiped away, joy fills their hearts as they
remember, "Our Lord is coming." Such was the hope
of the primitive Church founded not upon creeds, theological systems, but upon the words of Christ and the
doctrines of the Apostles. Let us go elsewhere, perhaps
to the great world city, Rome. Crowds are coming from
everywhere. They gather in one of the arenas, a great
amphitheatre, to witness a scene with which pagan Rome
frequently amused its callous multitudes. Christians, branded
as enemies of the gods of Rome and of the state, condemned
to death, are to meet the lions and the tigers. Others are
to be nailed to crosses, or to be consumed by fire. The
shouting, gesticulating hundreds and thousands have
gathered. Then a hush! A signal is given! Here they
come! Men, women and even children. They enter the
arena singing hymns of praise. One word is heard again
and again; they are shouting their "Maranatha!" Our
Lord is coming! They met the lions and the tigers, the fire
and the tortures with "that blessed hope." *Dr. Schaff*
in his excellent "History of the Church" has stated it
well.

"Christian Chiliasm (the thousand year reign of Christ
on earth) if we leave out of sight the sensuous and fanatical
extravagance into which it has frequently run, both in
ancient and modern times, is based on the unfulfilled promises
of the Lord, and particulary on the Apocalyptic statement
of *His thousand years' reign upon earth, after the first resurrection*, in connection with numerous passages respecting
His glorious return which declare it to be near, and yet
uncertain and unascertainable as to its day and hour, that
believers may always be ready for it. *This precious hope,
through the whole age of persecution, was a copious fountain of
encouragement and comfort under the pains of that martyrdom*

which sowed in blood the seed of a glorious harvest for the church."

How long this blessed hope, as well as the hope of the kingdom to come, was maintained in its Scriptural simplicity and purity we shall now follow. The so-called "Apostolic Fathers" who followed, were the mouthpieces of the hope of Christ's return and His thousand year reign. Many of these had Apostolic instructors and some had known the Apostles Paul and John. So *Barnabas*, in an epistle ascribed to him, says "Sabbath rest will come when the Son of God shall appear and destroy the lawless one. The true Sabbath is the Sabbath of the thousand years. Then all will be sanctified and completed, when we shall have become perfectly righteous, that is, when Christ comes back to reign." *Polycarp* had known John personally and received Christian teachings from the lips of the beloved disciple. He had a young disciple by name *Irenaeus*. He told him often what blessed fellowship he had with John. He also informed him of his conflict he had with a great Gnostic leader by name of *Marcion*. Gnosticism denied the resurrection, as well as the return of Christ, the judgment and much else. True to John's inspired instructions, when Marcion met Polycarp, he refused him the common greeting and said, "I know thee who thou art, thou firstborn of the devil" (2 John Verses 10, 11). Polycarp was a strong believer in Christ's glorious return and left this testimony behind, "If we obey Christ and please Him in this age, we shall receive the age to come (the millennial age). He will raise us up from the dead, and we shall live and reign with Him." As a very old man Polycarp refused to say "the emperor our Lord" to escape martyrdom. Before the fire at the stake was lighted he prayed, "Lord, Almighty God, Father of Thy beloved Son, Jesus Christ, through whom we have received from Thee the knowledge of Thyself; God of angels and of the whole creation; of the human race, and of the just that live in Thy presence; I praise Thee that Thou hast judged me worthy of this day and of this hour, to take part in the number of Thy witnesses, in the cup of

Thy Christ" (Neander Church History Vol. 1, pp. 110-111).

We should have mentioned in connection with Barnabas, *Clement.* We believe this is the Clement of Philippians iv:3, a fellow laborer with Paul. We have under his name, an epistle to the Corinthians and the fragment of a second. He gave witness of the speedy coming of Christ to set up His kingdom. As a close companion of Paul and John, Clement declared, "that the Apostles, assured by the resurrection of Christ, and confirmed by their converse with Him, all went forth proclaiming the good news, that the Kingdom of God was about to come, when the righteous are made manifest, and martyrs receive their reward from Him." Another companion of John and Polycarp was *Papias,* Bishop of the Church in Hierapolis, who lived in the first half of the second century. He was a man of sincere piety, but was of an easy credulity. His voluminous writings are lost. He evidently held some fanciful views as to the reign of Christ. *Eusebius,* the Church historian, a great opponent of the Premillennial view, wrote of him as, "well skilled in all manner of learning, and well acquainted with the Scriptures." Afterwards Eusebius describes him as "limited in comprehension," because he was a Premillennarian and taught with other contemporaries," that there will be a Millennium after the resurrection from the dead, when the personal reign of Christ will be established on the earth." *Ignatius,* Bishop in Antioch, whose writings are lost, no doubt bore a similar testimony. Then there was one named *Hermas,* whom some claim to be the Hermas of Romans xvi:4. He left a work entitled, "The Shepherd." He also looked forward to the time of the "Regeneration," following Christ's return and the resurrection of the just, "They shall obtain victory and reward, but the world that now is shall be destroyed by fire. This age is winter to the just, the future, coming age is summer."

In 1873 the Metropolitan of Nicomedia, in Asia Minor, discovered in the library attached to the monastery of the Most Holy Sepulchre, in the Greek quarter of Constantinople an interesting manuscript, the only one in existence. *Philetos*

Byrennios, the Greek Metropolitan, had it published. It is known as the *Didache*, the Teaching of the twelve Apostles." The Greek text and the English translation was published by Charles Scriber's Sons in 1885, a copy of which is in the author's possession. We quote the last chapter of this document, containing the belief of the church concerning the coming of the Lord, in the beginning of the second century, for the date of the *Didache* is probably around the year 140 or 150.

"Watch for your life's sake; let your lamps not go out, and your loins not be loosed but be ready; for ye know not when your Lord cometh. But ye shall come together often, and seek the things which will befit your souls; for the whole time of your faith thus far will not profit you, if ye be not made perfect in the last time.

For in the last days the false prophets and the corruptors shall be multiplied, and the sheep shall be turned into wolves, and love shall be turned into hate; for when lawlessness increases they shall hate one another, and shall persecute and deliver you up, and then shall appear the world-deceiver as a son of God, and shall do signs and wonders, and the earth shall be given into His hands, and he shall commit iniquities which have never yet been done since the beginning. Then all the race shall come into the fire of trial, and many shall be made to stumble and perish. But they that endure in their faith shall be saved from under even this curse. And then shall appear the signs of truth; first the sign of an opening in the heavens, then the sign of a trumpet's sound, and thirdly the resurrection of the dead, yet not all, but as it has been said—The Lord shall come and all the saints with Him. Then shall the world see the Lord coming upon the clouds of heaven."

In analyzing this interesting document we find at least ten facts founded on the Scriptures. (1) The impending character of the second coming of Christ and the duty of the Church to be ready and to watch for the imminent coming of the Lord. Here Matthew xxiv:42 is quoted. (2) The solemn duty of Christians to assemble together to promote

preparation for the promised return of the Lord. This is to
be the normal attitude of the Church. It refers us to
Hebrews x:25, 37. (3) The increase of false teachers in the
Church during the last days. Here we face the following
passages, Matthew xxiv: 5, 24; Second Thessalonians ii:1-8;
1 Peter ii-1-2. (4) Lawlessness together with hate and persecution, treachery, alienations, etc. will characterize Christendom in those days, preceding the coming of the Lord.
This confirms Matthew xxiv:24 and 2 Timothy iii:1-4. (5)
The apostacy is mentioned: "Many shall be made to stumble." See again Matthew xxiv:5, 24. (6) The coming of the
final, personal Antichrist, as a self deifying, Christ opposing,
Christ imitating, world deceiver, the man of sin full of
iniquities (Matthew xxiv:5 and 2 Thessalonians ii). (7) The
great tribulation out of which only those who endure faithfully, and to the end, shall be saved (See Dan. xii:1; Matt.
xxiv:21; Rev. 7:14). (8) The signs of the advent based upon
Matthew xxiv: 29-31; Revelations i:7; xix:11 and 1 Thessalonians iv:16-18. (9) The resurrection of the righteous
alone. John v:29; I Corinthians xv:23, etc. (10) The
glorious manifestation of the Lord, coming in the clouds of
heaven (Matt. xxiv:30; Acts i:2; Rev. i:7; xix:11-16).
What interests us the most is the fact that Matthew xxiv is
quoted seven times. Most expositors and commentators of
both Catholic and Protestant Christendom, claim that
Matthew xxiv had its fulfilment in the year 70 in the destruction of Jerusalem. They tell us Christ came then. What
preceded the destruction of city and temple was "the great
tribulation" and upon that they base their assertion that no
future tribulation needs to be expected. But the Church in
the second century did not believe this at all; they did not
teach a fulfilment of Matthew xxiv in the year 70; they did
not believe that Antichrist had appeared. They are waiting,
as we still do, for the fulfilment of the Olivet Discourse.
They believed then, as we still believe, that the return of
Christ will be preceded by a time of lawlessness, by the great
tribulation, and the manifestation of the man of sin. They
believed, as we still believe, that His coming will be visible,

personal and glorious.   Though the document does not enter
into the details of His return, yet we learn that they believed
in the first resurrection.   The *Didache* confirms the premillennial faith of the primitive church, given by the mighty
witnesses right after the Apostles had passed away.   As Dr.
Schaff says in his "Church History", "They shine with the
evening red of the Apostolic day, and breathe an enthusiasm
of simple faith and fervent love and fidelity to the Lord which
proved its power in suffering and martyrdom."   Polycarp,
Papias, Ignatius, Clement, Barnabas, Hermas, Hegesippus
and others were one in their belief that the Christ who had
died for them, the Christ whom they adored, the Christ for
whose sake they were martyred, is coming again, coming to
claim His dominion, coming to end the serpent's rule, coming
victoriously to end the conflict of the ages.   Age-long was
the battle, the enmity between the woman's seed and the
serpent's seed.   The seed of the woman will conquer!   The
great scholar of a past generation, *Dean Alford*, in his New
Testament annotations says, "The whole Church for the first
three hundred years understood Revelation xx:1-6 in a plain,
literal sense," and "that it is the most cogent instance of
unanimity which primitive antiquity presents."   It is true!
Church history has no consensus more unanimous for any
doctrine than is the consensus of the Apostolic fathers, whose
illustrious names we have mentioned above, for the premillennial coming of our Lord.   But we have not yet mentioned
the disciple of Polycarp, the friend of the Apostle John,
Irenaeus, though he cannot be classed among the Apostolic
fathers, but properly belongs to the Apologists.   He was an
able man, learned and deeply spiritual.   He wrote a book on
heresies, in the fifth part of it he defends strenuously the
premillennarian doctrine against the Platonizing Gnostics,
that plague of the early Church.   In writing of the prophecies
of Daniel, John and the words of Christ, he says, "Christ is
the stone cut out without hands, who shall destroy temporal
kingdoms, and introduce an eternal one—when Antichrist
shall have devastated all things in this world, he will reign for
three years and a half, and sit in the temple of Jerusalem,

and then the Lord will come from heaven in the clouds, in the glory of the Father, sending this man to the lake of fire, but bringing in for the righteous the times of the kingdom, the rest, the hallowed seventh-day, and restoring to Abraham the promised inheritance." We give two more quotations, "Christ Himself will renew the inheritance of the earth, and reorganize the mystery of the glory of His sons"; and again, "In the times of the kingdom, the *righteous shall bear rule* upon their rising from the dead, when the creation, having been restored, and set free, shall fructify with abundance of every kind, from the dew of heaven, and from the fertility of the earth." "In the times of the kingdom, the earth shall be called by Christ to its pristine condition, and Jerusalem rebuilt, after the pattern of the Jerusalem, which is the mother of us all." He bore repeatedly testimony to the resurrection of the Just and to the great white throne. He has been assailed by certain anti-millennialists as teaching sensuous, grossly fanciful things, branded as Jewish nonsense. It is true he had adopted some of the extravagant beliefs current in his day, but the fact remains, if we omit these fanciful things, that Irenaeus was a strong believer in the coming of Christ and the kingdom He will receive and establish. There can be no question whatever that in the post-Apostolic age, into the second, third and partly fourth centuries the Millennial belief was the accepted belief of the Church; those who denied it were the heretics, such as the Gnostics and others. The most painstaking historians bear witness to it. *Gibbon*, the brilliant author of "The Rise and Fall of the Roman Empire" was an infidel. He gave five reasons for the wide-spread progress of Christianity in the first centuries. Among these he places the unwavering faith in the Return of Christ.

CHAPTER II

The Testimony of the Apologists and other Witnesses of the Second and Third Centuries*

The opponents to the teachings of the Prophets, the Apostles, the Apocalypse and the Apostolic fathers, that there will be a second literal and personal Coming of Christ followed by His thousand years reign, claim that one of the originators of this interpretation was *Cerinthus*. Two outstanding sects harassed the Church in the first and second centuries. The first was the Judaizing sect, which the Holy Spirit completely answers in the Epistle to the Galatians. The other sect was known by the name of Gnosticism. Gnosticism (from the Greek word *Gnosis*, knowledge), was divided into numerous sects. It would take a whole volume to explain their philosophical, often fantastic, inventions. The Epistle to the Colossians answers their heresies, for the Christians in Colossae were greatly troubled by Gnostic teachers. In the second chapter of the Colossian Epistle we find a solemn warning against the insipient Gnosticism of that day. "Beware lest any man spoil you through *philosophy* and vain deceit, after the *tradition* of men, after the *rudiments* of the world, and not after Christ" (Col. ii:8).

Some of the later Gnostic sects attached themselves to Judaism, and taught a gradual development of the Theocracy among mankind from an original foundation of it in the race itself. Cerinthus and his teachings must be considered as the intermediate link between the Judaizing sects and the sects of Gnosticism. His Christology was heretical.

---

*The author has made research for years in Church History and in the early sources of Christianity. Of great help to him have been a series of lectures given in the first Prophetic Conference held in New York City in 1879. The author, then in his prime, was Dr. Nathaniel West, a man of the deepest scholarship, an excellent Hebrew and Greek scholar. We knew him well and thirty-eight and forty years ago we often spent hours together on controversial points in prophetic interpretation. He was an ardent Premillennialist. On some points we could not agree.

He, with the Ebionites, denied the supernatural conception of Christ. In common with the Ebionites, he traced back all divine attributes in Christ to the descent of the Holy Spirit at His baptism. Again Cerinthus agreed with the Ebionite heresy in teaching that the Mosaic law continues and Christians are bound to keep it. He also had adopted the view of a lower earthly Messiah, the man Jesus, who was only the vehicle and organ of that heavenly Christ, who wrought in the earthly Jesus. Cerinthus had no conception of Immanuel, God manifested in the flesh, the Son of God appearing in the form of a servant. And so he taught with other Jewish Theologians that Jesus, after having triumphed over every enemy, through the power of the heavenly Christ, united with him, would reign in the glorified Jerusalem, the central point of the glorified earth. From Psalm xc:4 he inferred the world would continue in its present condition for 6,000 years. At the close of this period would follow, he taught with others, a thousand years of sabbaths on earth, of uninterrupted blessedness, when the righteous shall be delivered from all their troubles and conflicts. It is doubtful that he taught the gross and sensual notions about that millennial sabbath held by the Ebionites and others. Such views were repugnant to the spirit of Gnosticism.

To charge Cerinthus with having invented the Millennium, after Christ's coming, Cerinthus with his hodge-podge of Judaism, Ebionitism and Gnosticism, is far from being the truth. It reveals the weakness of the school which is next to incurably antagonistic to Premillennialism. No! Not Cerinthus or others invented the kingly reign of Christ, after His return, but the Holy Spirit has revealed it. It grounds itself in the visions of Daniel and completes itself in the visions of John in Patmos. Daniel beheld the passing of the world-empires, the catastrophe when the final political conditions of the times of the Gentiles have been reached, when the striking stone does its work and becomes the kingdom that shall rise upon its ruins. By the same Spirit John, the beloved disciple, beheld some 600 years later the details of the coming of the Son of Man and portrays the steps by which it is reached, the events which precede the establishment of the kingdom. Between the two, Daniel's visions and John's vision of consummation we have the harmonious testimony of the Prophets of God, the confirming witness of the Lord Jesus Christ Himself, and the revelations given through Paul, Peter, John, James and Jude, a progressive revelation, culminating in the Apocalypse. On these sure and unshakeable foundations did the Apostolic Church built its doctrine of the Premillennial Advent of the Lord Jesus Christ in order to inaugurate the kingdom. The prophecies of Daniel were regarded as a calendar of the future, measuring the range of the successive Gentile world-powers from the days of Nebuchadnezzar to the finishing of the mystery of God under the seventh trumpet, after which come the recorded events, such as the overthrow of the two beasts, the masterpieces of Satan. Only after these events can the Son of Man come in the clouds of heaven to receive the kingdom. An allegorical or symbolical coming in the clouds of heaven was unknown in the early Church. "I challenge the opponents of these views to produce a single passage from any writers of authority in the first centuries, in favor of the modern figurative interpretation of Daniel vii:14, Matthew xxiv:30 and Luke xxi:27."*

But who were the men who began to question the authenticity of the Book of Daniel? Who were the men who tried to keep the Revelation from being accepted as the genuine work of the beloved disciple and tried their utmost to cast doubt upon it? Not the men who upheld Apostolic doctrines but those who rejected certain truths, notably the Alexandrian school, whose most important exponent was *Origen* with his Platonic Intellectualism. This school turned the symbols of the book of Revelation into mere metaphors, questioned its divine authority, invented another John, a certain elder, as the author, as well as the rationalistic

---

*Cunnighame of Lainshaw.

arguments, so widely used in our present day Modernism against the final book of the Bible. At the same time, Origen and his transcendental philosophy indirectly encouraged Gnosticism and well nigh wrecked the doctrine of the resurrection.

The Apostolic fathers were followed by the Apologists in the second century, men of piety and learning. We have already given to our readers the testimony of the disciple of Polycarp, Irenaeus, who must be reckoned among the Apologists. Some of them are silent on the question of the return of Christ and the kingdom. To infer from this, as it has been done, that they did not believe it, or teach it, is wrong. Scholars like Tatian, Athenagoras and others wrote specially against pagan mythology and philosophy and therefore omitted any reference to the Millennium. To interpret their silence as meaning they did not believe in it, as their colleagues did, is not reasonable.

One of the outstanding Apologists was *Justin Martyr*. He was born about the time the Apostle John died. He was of Roman descent, born of heathen parents in Palestine. He received a fine education in the leading schools of philosophy of his time. He was first a follower of the School of Stoicism; later he became a Platonist and finding that philosophy led nowhere, Justin became a Christian. He became one of the outstanding defenders of Christianity in the second century. His first "Apologia" was addressed to Emperor Antonius Pius. Fortunately one of his dialogues has been preserved. It is a dialogue between himself and a Jew by name of Trypho. We give part of it.

Trypho asked, "Do you believe that this place, Jerusalem, shall be rebuilt and your people be congregated and rejoice with Messiah (Christ) and the patriarchs and prophets?" This question Justin answered by saying, "I confessed to you before, that I and many others besides, do believe as you well know, this shall be. On the other hand, I have also signified to you that many, who are not of the pure and pious faith of the Christians, do not confess this. They are called Christians, indeed, but are godless, impious heretics, because they teach doctrines that, in every respect, are blasphemous, atheistic and foolish . . . they do not confess this, but dare to blaspheme the God of Abraham, Isaac and Jacob, and say there is no resurrection of the dead, but that at death souls are received into heaven. Do not imagine that these are Christians. But I and others who are orthodox on all points, know there will be a resurrection from the dead, and a thousand years in Jerusalem, built again, broadened and adorned, as the prophets Isaiah, Ezekiel and others declare. A certain man among us, of the name of John, one of the Apostles of Christ, in a Revelation which he had, prophesied that they who are faithful to our Messiah would accomplish a thousand years in Jerusalem, and after that the general, and to speak concisely, the final resurrection and judgment of all would take place." Anti-Chiliasts, opposing the thousand year reign of Christ on earth, have tried to break down Justin's testimony. But their attempts have failed.

Another witness of the second century is *Melito* of Sardis. He was evidently a very voluminous writer but only a few fragments have survived from which we learn that he believed definitely in the literal meaning of the thousand years under the reign of Christ. *Nepos* is still another outstanding witness. He was Bishop in Egypt and was acknowledged as a great scholar. He was a strong believer in a coming Millennium, held strictly to the literal interpretation of prophecy and was an outspoken opponent of Origen's theories. His work "*Elegchos Allegoriston*," an answer to Allegory, is lost. But it was considered an incontrovertible argument for Christ's earthly millennial reign. It seems it was mostly based upon the Apocalypse. An authority gives the information that he separated the resurrection of the just from the resurrection of the unjust, and put the second resurrection at the close of the Millennium. So great was the influence of his teachings that Dionysius of Alexandria complained that many neglected the Scriptures for the writings of Nepos. After his death the same Dionysius of the Alexandrian school attacked his writings. And

what more could we say of *Tertullian*. Quintus Septimus
Tertullianus was born in Carthage in 160 A. D.—his father
was a Roman Centurion. When he was about thirty-six
years old he accepted Christianity and began at once to
attack fearlessly Pagans, Jews and the Gnostics. He possessed great natural gifts and acquired a vast amount of
historical, legal, philosophical and antiquarian knowledge,
which may be learned from His writings. He fell in with the
Montanistic movement, but did not accept all the teachings
of Montanus. It is said that Tertullian supported Montanism on account of his dislike of the Roman clergy. He
was an ardent Premillennialist. He wrote a great book,
after he turned his back on Montanism, the title of it was
"The Hope of Believers"; it belongs to the lost books.
Cyprian, once a splendid lawyer of high social standing,
became an earnest believer, was a Premillennairan. So was
Commodian, *Methodius*, the martyr who gallantly fought
the destructive school of *Origen*, defending the resurrection
of the body; *Victorinus*, the martyr, *Gregory of Nyssa*,
Athanasius, and others, held strongly the same belief in
the coming of Christ to establish His kingdom on earth.

A great German scholar, Dr. Dorner, states that the
opening centuries of our age were predominantly eschatological. Well says the author of *Horae Apocalypticae* (Hours
in Revelation), *Elliott*, "all primitive expositors, except
Origen and the few who rejected the Book of Revelation,
were Premillennialists." And another painstaking and
accurate historian, *Gieseler*, in his church history says "Chiliasm is so distinctly and prominently mentioned that we
do not hesitate regarding it as the general belief of that age."
Joseph Mede, whom we shall quote later more fully, a splendid
godly scholar of the seventeenth century says, "Chiliasm
was the general belief of all orthodox Christians in the age
immediately following the Apostles, and none were known
to deny it but heretics, who denied the resurrection." Still
another, *Chillingworth* in his works, declares, "It was the
doctrine believed and taught by the most eminent fathers
of the age, next to the Apostles and by none of that age

condemned." Add to it the words of *Dr. Adolf Harnack* and you have a witness which is conclusive. "The earlier fathers, Irenaeus, Hippolytus, Tertullian, believed in chiliasm simply because it was a part of the tradition of the Church, and because Marcion and the Gnostics would have nothing to do with this conception. It is the same all through the third and fourth centuries with those Latin theologians who escaped the influence of Greek speculation. Commodian, Victorinus Pettavensis, Lanctantius and Suplicius Severus were all pronounced Millennarians, holding the very details of the primitive Christian expectation."

We must give just one more testimony—that of *Hippolytus.* He was a Bishop, but little more of him is known. "As neither Eusebius nor Jerome were able to name the city in which he was bishop, we can say nothing more definite in the matter" (Neander Church History, vol I, p. 681). He was the author of numerous works on a variety of subjects, exegetical, dogmatic, polemical and chronological. Among them is a treatise on the Antichrist and a commentary on the Book of Daniel. We quote from the latter work:

"The golden head of the image, and the lion, denoted the Babylonian (as recorded in Chapter ii and vii of Daniel); the shoulder and arm of silver, and the bear represented the Persians and Medes; the belly and thighs of brass and the leopard meant the Greeks, who held the sovereignty from Alexander's time; the legs of iron and the beast dreadful and terrible expressed the Romans, who hold the sovereignty at present; the toes of the feet, which were part of clay and part of iron, and the ten horns, are emblems of the kingdoms which are yet to rise; the other little horn that grows up among them meant the Antichrist in their midst; the stone that smites the earth and brings judgment upon the world is Christ. Speak with me, O blessed Daniel! Give me full assurance I beseech thee! Thou dost prophesy concerning the lion for thou wast a captive there. Thou hast unfolded the future regarding the bear, for thou wast still in the world, and didst see the things come to pass. Then thou speakest to me of the leopard; and whence canst thou know this, for thou art already gone to thy rest? Who instructed thee to announce these things, but He who formed thee in thy mother's womb? That is God, thou sayest. Thou hast spoken indeed, and not falsely. The leopard has risen; the he-goat is come, he hath smitten the ram; he hath broken his horns into pieces; he hath stamped upon him with his feet. He has been exalted by his fall; the four horns have come up. Rejoice, blessed Daniel! thou hast not been in error! All these things have come to pass. After this again thou hast told us of the beast, dreadful and terrible. It has iron teeth and claws of brass; it devoured and brake in pieces and stamped the residue with the feet of it. Already the iron rules. Already it subdues and breaks all in pieces; already we see these things ourselves."

There is no need of marshaling other witnesses. In our next chapter we shall examine the corruption of the doctrine by heretical movements, which taught a false Premillennialism of the utmost carnality. We shall show when the hope of the ages became dimmed and when it was ultimately given up and the causes which led to this denial.

CHAPTER III

The Perversion and Corruption of the Kingdom Hope

Every vital doctrine of the Word of God, made known to man by revelation of God, is the object of attack, misrepresentation, perversion, and corruption by that person, whom the Lord Jesus Christ calls a liar, the devil. "He was a murderer from the beginning, and abode not in the truth, because there is no truth in him. When he speaketh a lie, he speaketh of his own; for he is a liar, and the father of it" (John viii:44). He is the serpent of Genesis iii:15. From the beginning he strikes with his vicious fangs at the seed of the woman, His Person and His work. We have traced this conflict in a separate volume.*

All the great doctrines of the Word of God center in the Person of the seed of the woman, the Son of God manifested in the flesh, Immanuel. His first coming has revealed the love of God for a lost world. The Gospel of God, the good news, which God proclaims, because Christ died for our sins, and the blessed truths connected with that Gospel, is the great message for this present age. The second coming of Christ will reveal the glory and power of Christ. While in His first coming we see Him as the Lamb of God, in His second coming He will be manifested as the Lion of the tribe of Judah. In His first coming peace was made in the blood of the Cross; in His second coming He will be enthroned as Prince of Peace to speak peace unto the nations, which will be gathered into the kingdom. The truths centering in this second advent of Christ belong also to the most vital in Scripture. If there were no second coming, humanity would have to gaze into a future of despair.

It is therefore not strange that the serpent and the serpent's seed have done their utmost to pervert and to corrupt both the Good News of Salvation, and the Good News of the coming Kingdom. Even in the days of the Apostles, a counterfeit Gospel began its deadly work. In holy zeal the

---

*"The Conflict of the Ages."

Spirit of God pronounced the divine curse upon that counter-feit Gospel (Gal. i:6-9). The reason for a corrupted Gospel is that the arch-enemy of the Cross and its work, hates the work Christ has finished. This corruption continues throughout our age. In the same way he hates the return of Christ and the great hope connected with it. As he has done with the Gospel of God, so has he done with the core doctrines of the second advent and the future kingdom. He has perverted and corrupted them, produced a false, unscriptural chiliasm, linked with it damnable heresies so as to bring it in disrepute and made it obnoxious through its fanatical adherents, some of whom plunged into the most abominable immoralities. It is a strange fact that today the true teachings of the Word of God about Christ's return and His future reign over the earth are by many confounded with the fanaticism which appeared in the second century and which had a similar revival in different periods of the Church. Thus the real hope of Christ's return is first misrepresented and then opposed. Take for an example many of our loyal and beloved Lutheran brethren, especially those of the Missouri Synod, as well as others. They raise the cry of Chiliasm as if it were a heresy and think of the days of the Reformation, when Thomas Muenster and the entire Anabaptist movement attempted to set up a kingdom, certainly not of God, but of the devil, and practised all kinds of immoralities and viciousness. So it is still today, as we shall show later. Like the demon possessed damsel which had joined herself to the Apostles, uttering the truth in saying, "these men are the servants of the most high God, which show unto us the way of salvation" (Acts xvi:17), so we find in our times cults and sects, which teach certain truths, yet demons are active in them, teaching perverse things. Most of these cults are pronounced in their Premillennial belief. More of this later.

We find fanatical perversions of the future kingdom in certain Judaizing sects, especially the Ebionites, many of whom rejected the Virgin birth and other cardinal Christian doctrines, besides teaching many perverse, unscriptural views. They were believers in the coming of Christ. They lived in

130

THE HOPE OF THE AGES

the expectation of Christ's speedy return, to restore Jerusalem, and to re-establish the Theocracy there in surpassing splendor. All the Jewish inventions, expressed in certain apocalyptic literature, like the Testament of the twelve Patriarchs, and others, they transferred to the millennial kingdom of Christ. This produced a carnal hope with no foundation in Scripture.

Towards the middle of the second century a strange and powerful sect arose which wrought great harm. The founder was *Montanus*, Phrygian by birth, he came into prominence about the year 170. Montanus was evidently a born fanatic. He fell frequently into trances so often exhibited in modern Pentecostalism. When he came out of these he claimed divine inspiration. He and his followers believed in a continuance of miraculous gifts such as were in the Church during Apostolic days, hence he strenuously opposed the scriptural and logical view, that after Christianity had become established, sign gifts and miraculous manifestations ceased. Some of his followers believed that he was the Holy Spirit in person. He and his followers laid claim to a continued Pentecost. His principal associates with whom he traveled about were two women, who boasted of being prophetesses, Prisca (or Priscilla) and Maximilla. Later certain ecclesiastical writers accused Montanus of immorality. The learned Tertullian was misled and for a time supported Montanus and his fanaticism. He believed that Montanus was commissioned to complete the Christian revelation and esteemed him not inferior to the Apostles. It would require many pages were we to state all the heresies and inventions of this powerful movement, which for a time threatened the corruption of the Church. Montanus taught a grossly perverted Millennialism of a carnal type. All was steeped in materialism. Montanus believed that the village of Pepuza, in Phrygia was destined to be the seat of the millennial kingdom and not Jerusalem. He and his two female prophetesses had visions as to the nearness of Christ's coming. Thus the woman Maximilla declared at one time, "After me no prophetess shall arise, but the end shall come."

They believed in the gift of tongues also and in all kinds of miracles. "States somewhat akin to what occurred in pagan divination, phenomena like the magnetic and somnabulist appearances occasionally presented in pagan cults, were mixed in with the excitement of Christian feelings. Those Christian females who were thrown in ecstatic trances during public worship, were not only consulted about remedies for bodily ills, but also were plied with questions concerning the invisible world" (Neander, Church History Vol. I, page 520). Prophetic utterances were also given and setting of dates for Christ's coming. All was delusion and wild fanaticism.

According to Neander two causes led to a suppression of Chiliasm, on the one hand, the opposition to Montanism; on the other the influence proceeding from the Alexandrian school. The Montanists by their enthusiastic visions spread many fantastic pictures of things which would happen, which led many to take sides against the doctrine of the millennial kingdom. Caius, an presbyter of Rome, in his controversial tract against the Montanist Proclus, tried hard to stigmatize Chiliasm as a heresy set afloat, as we have stated before, by the detested Gnostic, Cerinthus. Caius considered the Revelation a book which Cerinthus had interpolated for the express purpose of giving credence to the doctrine. We cannot follow the controversy which arose in the third century over this doctrine, nor can we enlarge on Origen and his allegorization and spiritualization, still upheld in our own times in Roman Catholicism and Protestantism. The opposition increased rapidly and yet it did not fully succeed in downing the great hope of the return of Christ, and His coming kingdom.

The *Nicene Council* held and endorsed the martyr's doctrine, the hope of the Apostles, the Apostolic fathers and the Apologists. *Gelasius Cyzicus* a Greek historian in the fifth century took great pains in collecting the records of the Nicene Council, which had been scattered, mostly through the Arian war, so that an authentic copy was difficult to find. The above named historian brought them to light. The Bishops and pastors which gathered in the first half of the

fourth century met the attacks of over fifty years launched
by the Gnostic and Alexandrian schools. The authenticity
of the book of Revelation, the Apocalypse, had been questioned; some had rejected the book while others treated it
with suspicion. The Council held the Revelation to be
canonical, refused to eliminate it from the New Testament
and issued, what they termed "An ecclesiastical form"
(Diatyposis), in which is found the following confession and
teaching: "We expect a new heaven and earth, according to
the Scriptures, when the Appearing and Kingdom of the
great God and our Saviour, Jesus Christ shall have shone
forth. Then, as Daniel says, the Saints of the Most High
shall receive the Kingdom. Then the earth shall be pure
and holy, a land of the living and not of the dead, which
David, foreseeing, exclaimed, "I shall see the goodness of the
Lord in the land of the living." For, "Blessed" says Christ,
"are the meek, for they shall inherit the earth." These
Nicene words are indeed a living witness for the truth; they
still held in spite of the strong opposition. Whitby, in the
seventeenth century, the inventor of the deplorable Postmillennial theory, which has worked, and is still working
harm which cannot be estimated, which is responsible for
much of the destructive criticism, in his, "Treatise on Tradition," acknowledges the truth of the fact that Premillennialism was received by the Church of the beginning and
endorsed by the Nicene Council, he says, "It was received
not only in the Eastern part of the Church by Papias, Justin,
Irenaeus, Nepos, Appolinarius, Methodius, and in the West
and South by Cyprian, Victorinus, Tertullian, Lactantius,
and Severus, *but also by the Council of Nice.*" It is not true
as the present day opponents to Premillennialism claim,
"that it was *not* the faith of the Church of two centuries,"
and that its flourishing period, "was a brief one of about a
hundred years." We have given historical evidence which
disproves completely this assertion. The Premillennial faith
permeates the first three centuries of our age; though perverted through Montanism, denied by the Alexandrian school
of spiritualizing, it nevertheless continued to the Nicene

Council and beyond. Then came a period in the history of the Church when it disappeared entirely.

There is an important lesson in one of the kingdom parables of our Lord. In His parable of the ten virgins we find a miniature Church history. The ten virgins are symbolical of the entire Christian profession. Virgins typify the state of separation, such as is demanded of Christian believers. They had lamps, the vessels to give light; Christians are to be shining lights. They all went forth to meet the Bridegroom, expecting His return. A distinction is made between the true and the false, those who have oil and those who have not, the professing and the possessing. But the Bridegroom tarried; one century after the other passed and the expected One did not appear, Christ did not come back. Then the entire Christian profession began to slumber and to sleep. It has a very simple meaning, the hope of His coming was given up. The Person who had a large share in the abandonment of the hope, who was used as an instrument of the powers of evil to usher in a period of many centuries in which the primitive hope, the scriptural hope, the hope of the prophets, the hope of the Apostles and the early Church fathers was supplanted by a counterfeit, was Constantine, misnamed, the Great. Let church historians speak of him as an instrument of God to save the Church from Roman persecutions. We disagree! He was the very opposite. He opened wide the gate by his political-religious triumph, to all the corruptions which found their culmination in Roman Catholicism. The temporal supremacy of Christianity in the Roman Empire lulled the Church asleep and produced a new theory of the Millennium.

We have to check our pen. One could write a number of volumes describing the political history of the fourth century, showing how the Church gave up that separation which makes her a distinctive, a peculiar body, not of the world, and how after that separation was relinquished corruption after corruption followed, till that which claimed to be the Church of Christ became a sink of doctrinal perversion, moral corruption and all kinds of viciousness. We shall

make use of the eloquent words of Dr. Nathanael West, for we
feel that he describes these conditions in a satisfying way.*

"The martyr age had passed away. No more Councils like
that of Nice, in which martyrs, fresh from the Maximian
persecution, answered to their names. No Paphnutius any
more, venerable with silvery hair, one eye gouged out by
the tool of the pagan torturer, its frightful socket seared
with a red hot iron, both legs ham-strung, and standing
besides young Athanasius of only twenty-seven summers
defending the orthodox faith. A new generation had appeared, intoxicated with the Christian conquest of heathen-
ism, the careering splendor of the Church and state establishment, and whirling a mystic dance around the tranquility
of the empire."   Well writes Kurtz in his Church History:
"As the aspect of outward affairs changed under Constantine,
these views (Christ's coming kingdom by His return) lost
their hold on men's minds. The Church now prepared for
a long continued period of temporal prosperity, and the
State Church forgot the millennial glory of the future."
And the great premillennial expositor, the German scholar
Bengel in his commentary on the Revelation written several
centuries ago, says: "When Christianity became a worldly
power, the hope of the future was weakened by the joy over
the present success." Another German scholar, writing on
Daniel, declared, "Chiliasm disappeared in proportion as
Papal Catholicism advanced. The Papacy took to itself,
as a robbery, that glory which is an object of hope. . . . When
the Church became a harlot, she ceased to be the Bride
who goes to meet her Bridegroom, and thus Chiliasm disappeared" (Auberlen on Daniel). The whole story can be
given in a nutshell. With the coming of Constantine, the
Church became a world-institution, Christians began looking at the existing temporal prosperity as fulfilling the
prophecies, and then ceased to look for the promised return
of Christ.

"A new theory of the Millennium came rapidly to the

_____
*"Prophetic Conference Report."   Page 348.   New York, 1879.

foreground. The vision of Daniel in chapter seven and John's vision in the nineteenth and twentieth chapters were now explained as referring to the *first* coming of Christ and not to His *second*. The Millennium was therefore believed to be a present fact. The cross, once a symbol of ignominy, the *Infelix Lignum*, the tree of misery, became the emblem of honor."* We find it on Roman standards, the soldiers shields, the priestly robes, on the so-called altars of the Church; it became an object of worship, adoration, all plain idolatry; the crown which belongs to Him, more than a crown, the many diadems, was forgotten and no longer mentioned. All kinds of error-doctrines sprang up. A few drops of water sprinkled or poured upon a baby, produces regeneration and carries with it the assurance of salvation. Crowned neophytes, arrayed in white robes, with palm branches in their hands, surround the altar, while priests chant the 'new song'." All the Old Testament prophecies respecting Israel were claimed in their fulfilment by the empire of the fourth century. The promised thousand year reign of Christ following, according to Scripture, the second advent were now ingeniously slipped back and dated from the birth and ministry of Christ. The binding of Satan too is no longer in the future, the abyss in which he is shut up means, "the non-Christian nations." The thrones of Judgment are the unseen benches of the unseen twelve Apostles. The thousand year reign is an accomplished fact! The Millennium has come! The reign is partly ecclesiastical in the Romish church; partly temporal in the control of politics; partly ceremonial through the "sacraments" and partly heavenly, so far as it relates to the blessedness of the righteous in heaven. This is the first resurrection. Such was the now predominant belief. The future Millennium, the hope of the martyrs, the hope of all the earth as well, to be realized, according to the Scriptures, at the second advent, was grossly spiritualized into a present politico-religious fact. Origen had begun this spiritualizing, but *Augustinus* is the

---

*Dr. Nathaniel West.

man responsible for this perversion, a perversion which is now so widely adopted in Protestant Christendom. His greatest work he left is *De Civitate Dei*, The City of God. He says that he had once held to the Millennium as the great future Sabbath. He did not consider the doctrine objectionable, provided the joys of the righteous are figured as spiritual. But, proceeding to discuss the subject, he advocated the proposition, *that the earthly kingdom of Christ is the Church*, which he claimed was even then in the millennial era, and on the road to a glorious ascendency over all its enemies. This deadly error that the Church of Jesus Christ is His earthly kingdom, when the Holy Spirit *nowhere* teaches this, is proclaimed from thousands of pulpits in Protestant Christendom and has been, and still is, the most subtle, as well as successful, barrier in keeping Christians away from a real knowledge of the purposes of God; likewise is it responsible in greater part for wrong doctrines, for the carnalization of the Church, for its degradation and prostitution in going into all kinds of social reforms and besmearing itself with the politics of the world. And today in spite of the most solemn evidences in world events, confirming Bible prophecy, revealing an astonishing, almost sweeping increase of Atheism and Antichristianity, as well as apostasy in nominal Christendom, the Augustinian invention, that the Church is the kingdom, that the Church must advance the earthly kingdom of Christ and bring all nations into it, still prevails. Surely the god of this age has blinded their eyes.

Well says Dr. West, "By union of Church and State, the martyr doctrine itself was martyred, the truth was rejected, no council resisting, and vanished from view with the departing glory and last remnant of a suffering, but pure Apostolic Church." Then came two panics. The first in the sixth century. According to the erroneous chronology of the Septuagint version of the Bible, the imagined six thousand years ending with the destruction of the earth and with judgment, had expired; a panic followed, but it did not last very long. It was different when the year

1000 A.D. arrived. Now surely Christ had reigned a thousand years. Kings, princes, noblemen of every sort, peasants, rich and poor, all were panic stricken and filled with terror. They expected that the heavens would be rolled away like a scroll, that Gabriel would sound His trumpet, that all graves would be opened and the great White Throne set up, after which heaven and earth would pass away. The *Dies Irae*—the day of wrath—was now at hand. The Pope, Bishops, and Priests exhorted the people to be ready. The rich were told to give everything to the "Church," as if the Church would have any use for it, after the destruction of the world. But that was the time when the Papacy gathered up immense riches, when monasteries became institutions of wealth as well as of corruption. The panic was so great that enemies became speedily reconciled, all charters were executed in view of the nearness of the end of the world, wars were prohibited and many businesses were suspended. Well, the trumpet did not sound, no grave was opened, and the heavens remained as they were. Nobles and rich men had become poverty stricken, and the successor of the fisherman of Galilee, Peter, became loaded down with an abundance of gold and silver which our beloved brother Peter not even dreamed of, for he had none (Acts iii:6). After the delusion was over the darkness became denser. Someone invented the idea that the right date from which the thousand year reign of Christ in His kingdom in the Church should be dated from the victory of Constantine in the year 312 A.D. So the end of the world was postponed to 1312. When the Mohammedan hordes were invading Europe and wrought great havoc, they were put down as being Gog and Magog of Revelation xx:8. Another brief panic followed in which the Flagellants appeared, scourging themselves till the blood flowed freely, and exhorting the people to repent. When the fourteenth century had come and gone the general opinion was expressed that the one thousand years must be looked upon as a period of time of indefinite duration. Then came into greater prominence the Lateran doctrine, that the Papacy is "the kingdom of Christ," Daniel's fifth monarchy, the smiting stone of the second chapter of Daniel, Christ reigning on earth in the person of His visible head and representative, the Pope, was now taught. Such was the confusion worse confounded after the true doctrine of Christ's return and His visible reign had been given up.

CHAPTER IV

The Morningstars of the Reformation and the Witness of the Reformers

Going back to the early centuries and their stalwart witnesses, we find that interpreters of the Book of Revelation applied the 1260 days (Rev. xi:3) to the pagan persecutions which the Church had to undergo; the Babylon of Revelation (chapters 17 and 18), was for them pagan Rome, the seven hilled city and they looked upon certain emperors as the predicted Antichrist. When the true Scripture teachings as to the personal and glorious return of Christ to receive the millennial kingdom and to reign for a thousand years had been given up, very little was heard about the Antichrist. The Papacy had become more arrogant, sinking deeper and deeper into apostacy, into licentiousness and an almost indescribable viciousness. Some of the Popes were monsters in human form. Bishops, Abbots, Priests, and other ecclesiastics, with a lip confession of celibacy kept their concubines, lived open lives of harlotry and shame, seducing wherever they could. Books like *Gesta Romanorum*, Boccacio's "Decameron" and others brought to light the vicious immoralities of priests and monks; the invented "confessional" was used to corrupt and to seduce. Gradually but surely voices were raised against those things and fingers pointed to Papal Rome, as the Babylon of Revelation and to the Pope as the Antichrist. The first feeble steps were done to bring about a revival of the forgotten hope and the true meaning of Christ's millennial reign. The Roman Church is Babylon! The Man at Rome is the Antichrist! The Bishop of Orleans, in the council of Rheims, cried out, "O wretched Rome! wallowing in vices! Thy Pontiff seated on a throne, clad in purple and gold! He is the Antichrist sitting in the Temple of God, and demeaning himself as a god." Another witness points to Rome and called it "Satan's seat." Olivi, Ubertino, and a hundred more of Italy's choicest sons branded the Pope as "the new Lucifer," bedecked with gold, sitting in the Temple of God. They all perished on the

scaffold. Immortal Dante called him the "Modern Pilate."
Then Papal Rome began to outdo pagan Rome in torture
and the most awful bloody persecutions. Mighty witnesses
arose then, as the morningstars of the Reformation. We
must listen to some of their voices.

One of the outstanding morningstars which twinkled in
the dawn of the Reformation, when the darkness of the
Middle Ages was nearly over, was *Wyckliff*. He was born in
the year 1324 in the village of Wyckliff in the County of
York. He studied philosophy and theology in the University of Oxford. Christians who are not acquainted with
the story of his life have missed much. It is out of our reach
even to touch upon the highpoints of his remarkable career
as a reformer. He fairly raved against the transubstantia-
tion blasphemy. He represents Satan saying, "If by my
representative, the Antichrist (the Papacy), I can so far lead
astray the faithful of the Church, that they shall hold this
sacrament to be no longer bread, but an abominable acci-
dent, I shall by that very thing lead them afterwards to believe whatever I will." He denounced the Papacy and its
corrupting influences. What great truths he uttered! "Holy
Church," he says, "is the assembly of just men for whom
Christ shed His blood, and not mere stones, and timber, and
earthly dross, which *the priests of Antichrist* magnify more
than the righteousness of God and the souls of men." The
Pope was for him the chief Antichrist. "The Pope is the
chief Antichrist who falsely pretends that he is the most
immediate vicar of Christ"; and in one of his last sermons we
find this noble confession, "So long as Christ is in heaven, the
Church has in Him the best Pope, and that distance hinder-
eth Him not in doing His deeds, as He promiseth that He is
with His own always, even unto the end of the world. We
dare not put two heads, lest the Church be a monstrosity."
The following words are a prophecy of the Lutheran Reformation which came true almost two centuries later. "I sup-
pose that some brothers, whom God may vouchsafe to teach,
will be devoutedly converted to the primitive religion of
Christ and abandoning their false interpretations of genuine

Christianity, after having demanded or acquired for themselves permission from Antichrist, will freely return to the original religion of Christ; *and they will build up the Church like Paul.*"

Equally great, in some respects even greater than Wyckliff are the bright stars which arose on the horizon of the fourteenth century in Bohemia, the Spirit-led forerunners of John Huss. As fascinating as the story of Wyckliff is the life of *John Militz* (or Milicz), who lived in Moravia. He was a great and eloquent preacher, preaching sometimes five times daily. Multitudes from everywhere came to hear him. His themes were taken largely from the Prophets and the Book of Revelation, and the greatest burden of his discourse was the Antichrist. In 1367 the Pope returned from Avignon to Rome, and Militz resolved to visit him. The Pope's arrival was delayed. Militz, obedient to what he called, the Spirit's voice, nailed on the church door of St. Peter, "The Antichrist has come." One of his leading books is the one entitled, "*De Antichristo.*" He was an ardent student of the Bible and paid special attention to the signs of the times, comparing them with the prophecies of the Old Testament, the Olivet Discourse and the prophecies in the Pauline Epistles. He predicted a revival for the Church in preparation of the second coming of Christ. Here are some of his words on "the abomination of desolation" which our Lord mentions in His last discourse (Matt. xxiv:15). "Where Christ speaks of the abomination in the temple He bids us to look around and observe how, through the negligence of her pastors, the Church lies desolate; just as, by the negligence of its pastors, the synagogue lay desolate. Iniquity has taken the upper hand. Has not love grown cold?" Then he pictured the ecclesiastical corruptions of his times, the corruption of society and brands it all as the work of the Antichrist. "When I consider all this, I said to the Spirit, which spake in me, Who is Antichrist? And He answered, there are many Antichrists." He who denies Christ, and His authority, is an Antichrist. The appearance of Antichrist in his opinion, was not a thing of the future, but was already a present fact.

Then we notice the strange interpretations he gave. For
instance, the angels, whom Christ was to send forth, to gather
up the tares for the burning of the last judgment, were the
preachers of divine truth, who are sent forth before the
second advent, to attack and to destroy the reign of Antichrist. At the same time Militz was deeply interested in the
lost. Scores of prostitutes were converted and brought back
from their lives of shame. In Prague a chapel to Mary
Magdalene was erected, and buildings were provided for the
residence and support of hundreds, if not thousands, of girls
and women, who had returned to virtue.

Another strong witness and forerunner of John Huss was
Matthias Janow, the son of a Bohemian knight. Most refreshing is his testimony: "Once my mind was compassed by
a thick wall; I thought of nothing but what delighted the eye
and the ear, till it pleased the Lord Jesus to draw me as a
brand from the burning. . . . I began to admire the truth in
the Holy Scriptures, to see how, in all things, it must be
exactly fulfilled; then I first began to wonder at the deep
wiles of Satan, to see how he darkened the minds of all, even
of those who seemed to think themselves the wisest." And
how he flayed the priests! He wrote, "And the Lord sent me
His Spirit who shoots the fire in my bones and into my heart,
leaving me no rest till I expose the hidden shame of the
mother of harlots" (Rev. xvii). He too saw in the Pope the
Antichrist. We could fill many pages with his scathing
words of rebuke and denunciation. The prediction in
2 Thessalonians, chapter two, that the falling away should
come first, Janow supposed was then already in force. He
also attacked the distinction made by the Romish hierarchy
between clergy and laity and taught that all believers are a
priesthood.

Then appeared the mighty witness, *John Huss*. He
descended from a very poor family, born in 1369. He
received a thorough education and built upon the foundations
laid by Militz and Janow, confirming, strengthening, and
enlarging their testimony. An equally great influence over
him were the writings of John Wyckliff. Huss himself

declares in a paper, composed about the year 1410, that since 1381, the writings of Wyckliff were read in the University of Prague, and that he had been studying them for more than twenty years. He attacked the Papal authority and called the Pope, "the vicar of Judas Iscariot." In his work on *De Ecclesia* he divided the clergymen, or priests, into two classes, the clergy of Christ and the clergy of the Antichrist. And later he wrote the following strong words, "the Pope and his prophets, the masters, teachers, and jurists, under the hypocritical name of holiness, conceal the abomination of the beast and the Papacy is the abomination of self-deification in the holy place." He expected that the emperor and the princes of his times would stand by him in his efforts as reformer, but was sadly disappointed. Then he saw in this a fulfilment of Revelation, that the kings would commit fornication with the great whore of Babylon, for they had fallen away from the truth of Christ, and embraced the lies of Antichrist. Faithful unto death, the horrible death of being burned alive, he obtained the martyr's crown, and so did his friend *Jerome of Prague*, who gave the same staunch testimony against the Antichrist, the Papacy. Others who witnessed against the Papacy were greatly stirred by the frightful ravages of the black death, by which hundreds of thousands were swept away. They turned to the prophets, and especially to the Revelation for the study of the signs of the times. Says Neander, "And so it came about that many thought they saw very near at hand the coming of Antichrist and the second advent of Christ. . . . Out of all this proceeded, on the one hand, divers movements of a fanatical spirit, and on the other, contemplations of a more sober and profound Christian seriousness." It was at this time the friends of God arose in Germany, John Tauler, Henry Suso and others. Before us on our table lies open the first edition of John Tauler's sermons, printed in 1498. In vain do we look through the volume to find any reference to Antichrist or the Revelation. The friends of God were given to introspection, the inner life. They were not seriously concerned about the kingdom to come, Christ's reign on earth, but they spoke of "the kingdom within." They yielded in a passive obedience to the ecclesiastical powers and none of them were concerned about the Antichrist. It is noteworthy that these witnesses came out of the Romish night, Wycliffe, Militz, Janow, Huss, Savanarola and scores of others, and after the study of Revelation pointed their accusing finger at the Papacy and the Romish Church, branding them as Antichrist and Babylon.

It was on October 31 in 1517 when an Augustinian monk, *Dr. Martin Luther*, stood before a church door in Wittenberg and nailed a significant document to the door, his famous ninety-five theses. That hammering was heard throughout Christendom. Luther aimed mostly at the vicious and blasphemous sale of indulgences by John Tetzel, one of the biggest frauds in history. Luther thundered away at the fraud—"The Pope's indulgences cannot take away sins, God only remits sins." In a short time all Germany was astir. But we are not writing a church history. We are tracing the gradual recovery of prophetic truths, of the second coming of Christ and the divinely promised establishment of His kingdom, the thousand year reign over the earth. What then do we hear from Luther's lips and pen? He bears the same witness as John Huss, Wycliffe, and many others; Rome is Babylon, the Babylon of the book of Revelation, the man with the Tiara, the triple crown, is not Christ's Vice Regent on earth; he is the predicted Antichrist. Luther did not mince matters; we shall not repeat here the "choice names" he used in denouncing the "holy father" and the whole Roman hierarchy. Rome tried hard to silence him, as Rome had silenced Huss and hundreds of other faithful witnesses. Of Papal Rome it is written, "And in her was found the blood of prophets, and of saints, and of all that were slain upon the earth" (Rev. xviii:24). Luther's blood was not added. A miraculous divine providence watched over him. As the great instrument of the Spirit of God he was, he continued and defied the deified imposter in Peter's chair in Rome. What did Luther believe about the return of Christ and the time it will take place? We have studied three sermons by Luther which give his belief. (I) *Ein trostlich Predigt von der Zukunft Christi*—a comforting sermon on the coming of Christ; Strassburg, 1536. (II) *Ein christlich und beweysung von den juengsten Tag, und seine zeichen, das er nicht vern met sein mag*—a Christian argument about the last day and its signs, that it cannot be far away; about 1520. (III) *Zwo predigt auff die Epistel S. Pauli*—Luther's sermon over the body of Duke Frederick of Saxony, text 1 Thess. iv:16-18; 1525. (IV) *Offenbarung des Endchrists aus den Propheten Daniel Wittenberg*, 1525.—The revelation of Antichrist from the Prophet Daniel.

In these sermons Luther repeatedly mentions the Pope as the predicted Antichrist. Furthermore Luther believed that the day of the Lord was not far away; he did not predict better things for Germany, but spoke of the "Abfall," the apostasy, again and again, predicting that matters would go from bad to worse. Here are his own words, "Some say that before the last day the whole world will become Christian. This is a falsehood forged by the devil, that he might darken sound doctrine, that we might not rightly understand it. Beware therefore of this delusion." So Luther did not share the delusion of Augustinus that the Church is the kingdom and that her work is to gather all nations into it before the last day. Nor did John Calvin believe it, for in his commentary on Matthew (Matt. xxiv:30), he says, "There is no reason why any person should expect the conversion of the world; for, at length, when it will be too late, and yield them no advantage, they shall look on Him whom they have pierced." John Knox also joins his solid voice to bear the same witness, "To reform the whole face of the earth is a thing that will never be done until *the King and Judge appears for the restitution of all things*." This certainly is Premillennialism. Many more similar witnesses could be added, born by the men of the Reformation. Philip Melanchton in his "*In Danielem Prophetam commentarius*," his commentary on Daniel, bears witness to the coming of Christ. We also mention Buchenhagen, Justus Menius, Adler, Rhegius, Osiander, Westphal and many other co-laborers of Martin

Luther, who shared the same belief. They all thought the thousand year reign of Christ was over, the end of the world was near and they looked for the speedy coming of Christ to destroy the Antichrist, the Papacy, and to introduce the state of eternal glory. Something happened in the early days of the Reformation which brought to the foreground once more the delusion and fanaticism of a false Millennialism, the corrupt Chiliasm of the early Church as taught and upheld by the Ebionites, the Montanist movement and others. It was the devil's work to keep Luther and other reformers from seeing and accepting the primitive belief of the Church as to Christ's return and the real blessed hope, and the truth about the future Millennium. The first was *Thomas Muenster*. He, Storch and others headed a band of fanatics, which had twelve apostles and seventy-two disciples and became known as "the prophets of Zwickau." He inaugurated the peasants war. He attempted to set up a new kingdom based upon misinterpretation of Scripture, especially the Revelation. Terror reigned throughout Germany and for a time threatened the Reformation.

A battle was fought on May 15, 1525 and Muenster and his adherents were completely defeated. Then came the *Anabaptists*, called so because they baptized by immersion. They attempted by fire and sword to set up a secular kingdom, as the kingdom of Christ, all without any regard to the teachings of the Word of God. Viciousness and all kinds of immoralities and crimes prevailed. We pass over the terrible blasphemies which marked the movement till the ringleaders fell victims to the torture and suffered the just penalty of their wild fanaticism. The entire Anabaptist movement disappeared. Later similar movements of wild fanaticism arose elsewhere, among those the French prophets of Dauphiny, and afterwards in the time of Cromwell the Fifth Monarchy men, they and others claimed falsely support from the book of Revelation. It was purely the devil's work. These fanatical outbreaks were used to discredit any kind of prophetic interpretation and people were warned against believing in a millennium of righteousness, glory and peace, as taught in the Bible. The seventeenth article of the famous "Augsburg Confession" was aimed not at the Scriptural view of the kingdom, but against the Anabaptists and their outrages. "The Augsburg confession, so far from being a polemic against it, only favored it, " as Lange remarks, "it negatives the assumption of a Millennium before the coming of Christ, as well as repels the idea of a "secular kingdom." Nothing is clearer than that the Reformers, when drawing up the Augsburg Article, repudiated the mediaeval view and "opened the way," as Ebrard says "for *a future correct view.*" "If according to that Article," says Steffann, "the pious shall have no earthly kingdom *before* the resurrection, then is not only Luther's view wrong, who dated the thousand year reign from Constantine, but every other view is condemned, which locates the Millennium either in the past or in the present."

So says another scholar, Koch, in His "Thousand Year Reign," "Against the Anabaptist conception of the thousand year kingdom, and *only* against that, was the Article of the Augsburg confession directed, which rejected the later Jewish opinion." In his book "For Chiliasm," Hebart makes the same statement: "Only those opinions were assailed in the Augsburg article, as they were spread abroad in the times of the Reformation, the carnal representations of the Anabaptists, and rightly rejected because they have nothing in the Scriptures for them, but everything against them." Still another German theologian, Rinck, shows that both the Helvetic and Augsburg confessions intended nothing more than a rebuke of the "demonic caricature of the hope of the primitive church fathers . . . " "We have therefore to dismiss the erroneous impression made in various histories of doctrine which seem to teach when using the vague word "Millennarianism," that the Reformed Symbols condemned the doctrine of the Premillennial Advent of Christ. What we do find is the condemnation of a false Chiliasm (as exhibited in the Anabaptist movement and others), but not a syllable against the true, and the solid basis laid for the necessary and irresistible conclusion of the Pre-Millennial Advent, a dogmatic position that not only sustains, but requires, the literal exegesis of the first resurrection."* We have made this quotation from Dr. West's lecture for the sake of many Lutheran and Reformed brethren who labor under the misconception that the Helvetic and Augsburg confessions branded Premillennialism a heresy.

At the same time there came to pass a premillennial revival in Great Britain. Cranmer, Hopper, Latimer, Ridley, Bucer, Peter Martyr and others including Bradford, were strong believers in the hope of His coming. Here are *Latimer's* words, "Let us cry unto Him day and night, Most merciful Father, *Thy Kingdom come.* Antichrist is known throughout all the world. The man or woman who can say with faithful heart these words 'Thy Kingdom come,' desireth in very deed that God will come to judgment, and *amend all things in this world*, and pull down Satan, that old serpent, under our feet." *Cranmer* composed an Anglican Catechism. Here is what he says in explaining the petition "Thy Kingdom Come": "We ask that His Kingdom may come, for that, as yet, we do not see all things put under Jesus Christ. We see, not yet, how the Stone cut out of the mountain without human labor, and which broke in pieces and reduced to nothing the image described by Daniel, or how the Rock, which is Christ, possesses and obtains the empire of the world given to Him by the Father. As yet, Antichrist is not slain. Whence it is that we desire and pray that, at length, it may come to pass and be fulfilled; *and that Christ alone may reign with His saints according to the divine promises and live and have dominion in the world.*" Thus gradually the dark night was giving way to the increasing dawn of a new day in which the Church was led back by the Word and the Spirit of God to "that blessed hope." But the midnight cry, "Behold the Bridegroom!" was not heard during the days of the Reformation.

---

*Nathaniel West, in "History of Premillennialism."

CHAPTER V

The Remarkable Developments During the Seventeenth and Eighteenth Centuries

As we have shown the great men preceding the Reformation, and the Reformers themselves, had much to say of Antichrist and his rule. In their conception the Antichrist was the Papacy, an interpretation which no well informed student of prophecy follows today. Two facts impress one very much in studying the prophetic witness of these centuries. We hear nothing about "that blessed hope," nothing about Him who is the great Hope, nothing about that face to face meeting, nothing about the greetings of joy of the first century—"Maranatha," our Lord is coming. As it is the case with morbid minds today, they were more occupied with Antichrist than with Christ, the glorified head of His body, the Bridegroom of the Church, His Bride. The judgment aspect and the fast approaching last day were emphasized. Only towards the close of the sixteenth century we hear voices which speak of the other side, Christ coming to reign, the reign of the Saints and a glimmer of the true hope was now and then seen, mostly in the English Reformation.

The second fact is still more significant. We hear nothing about Israel, the seed of Abraham, nothing about the promises given by God to His peculiar people, nothing about their future spiritual and national restoration. Their hope was forgotten, remained unmentioned; yet God's purpose concerning Israel is the key to the treasure house of prophecy, the solution of world problems. No true Christian can think God's own thoughts over with Him, unless he knows Israel's calling and destiny of earthly glory in the kingdom to come. To this we have to add another sorrowful fact. The pages of history covering the fourteenth, fifteenth, and sixteenth centuries record the most awful persecutions of the Jews. Periodical attempts were made to exterminate that race, and wipe it off the face of the earth. No historian can tell us how many hundreds of thousands were cruelly slaughtered during these dark centuries. They were accused of poisoning the wells, producing the "black death," of ritual murder, killing children to obtain their blood for their feast days, they were even blamed for catastrophes in nature, such as floods, earthquakes, and violent storms. They were tortured in the most cruel way, deprived of their possessions, of their children, and of their livelihoods. Fire and sword were to drive them to become "Christians." The persecution of the Jews during the Middle Ages is one of the darkest blots which disfigures the pages of the history of Christendom. Even the reformers had no use for them. Luther was a great man of God, but his intolerant spirit, his harsh and condemning words he heaped upon the Jews, were his disgrace.

And why such persecutions of that people? Why did Luther and many of his followers despise the Jews as a people? Because of ignorance. They lacked the deeper insight into God's purposes. They forgot that "Salvation is of the Jews." They knew nothing of the different ages. They followed the delusion of Augustinus that "the promised kingdom is the Church." Israel had no future save in that spiritual kingdom, in which all their national promises and hopes were falsely declared to be realized. If they had known the Scriptures, if Luther and many others had seen and believed the fact, so plainly stated in the Epistle to the Romans, "that God has not cast away His people," if they had read and believed what Paul revealed as to their coming conversion and national greatness in the real, Scriptural kingdom, they would have acted in a different way and would have received the real light and understanding of prophecy.

It is the same today. The land of Luther is swept today by the dirty waves of Antisemitism. Hitler, Goering, Rosenberg, the deluded leader of a special brand of Germanic Antichristianity, raving against the Jews, attempt the impossible. Not to speak of God's infallible Word, history should teach these modern Hamans a lesson. All the persecutions of the Middle Ages did not make an end of the Jew.

They survived; the Spirit of God had announced their survival in the Bible. They will also survive the Antisemitism of the twentieth century. But why such persecutions? Because of ignorance. If the place of Israel in God's program of redemption were known, the Antisemitism of professing Christendom would soon be curtailed.

We turn now to the developments in the seventeenth century. A great change came and Premillennialism forged to the front. "Men distinguished for learning and piety, whose luster adorned the prominent universities, and whose eloquence charmed all hearts, proclaimed the premillennial return of Christ," says rightly Dr. West. We can mention a very few names: *Burton*, *Archer* of London, *Burnett*, the Church historian, *Lange*, *Hebart*, *Worthington* and *Lavater* were staunch believers in the second coming of Christ to receive the kingdom. In Germany arose the Pietist movement, producing the *Berlenburg Bible*, a reference Bible on the same style as the Scofield Bible, though at least ten times as large, giving sound premillennial annotations, widely used during the seventeenth century and opening the eyes and hearts of thousands. *Spener*, *Petersen*, *Francke*, and *Thomasius* with many others proclaimed the hope of His coming in a way unknown to the Reformers. *John Milton* in England believed in His return. At the close of his brochure "Reformation in England" he broke forth in an outburst of praise and exaltation of Christ", *the eternal and shortly expected King.*"

It was a great day when in 1660 the English Baptists presented to Charles II a document. It was their premillennial confession. *John Bunyan*, the immortal author of "Pilgrim's Progress," was among those who signed the confession. Here it is: "We believe that Christ, at His second coming, will not only raise the dead, and judge and restore the world, but also take to Himself His kingdom, which will be a universal kingdom, and that, in this kingdom, the Lord Jesus Christ will be the alone Lord and King of the whole earth." How many pages we could fill with the witnesses of Scotland and the so-called "Westminster Divines"! Principal Baillie, who strenuously opposed the doctrine of Premillennialism, attending the Assembly in Scotland, grieved over the fact that the greatest members of the Assembly were Premillennialists. Among them was the prominent Calvinist *Dr. William Twisse.* Here are Dr. Baillie's words: "Most of the chief divines here, not only independents, but others, as Dr. Twisse, Marshall, Palmer, and many others, are express Chiliasts." The Westminster Assembly did not repudiate Premillennialism, as it is so often claimed. In the "Westminster Standard," Rome is papal, not Pagan; Antichrist is the Pope, not Nero; His Coming is personal and visible, not spiritual; the breath of the Lord's mouth which slays the wicked one, is judicial and not evangelical. "This generation" that passes not away, is not merely the generation then living but the continuous Jewish race. The one thousand years are not named precisely inasmuch as they are not named by Daniel, Christ, or Paul but are implicated throughout. "Any argument drawn from the silence, or non-mention of the one thousand years by the "Standards" against the truth of the premillennial advent, is an argument against the canonicity of the Apocalypse, which is not silent, but mentions these years, uncovering only what is elsewhere concealed or pre-intimated." (1 Cor. xv:23, 24")* Without entering into the details of the Westminster Assembly and Confession and the proof that they definitely taught that Christ's coming is before the Millennium, we call attention to the fact that the true, godly and learned witnesses of the premillennial coming of Christ of the seventeenth century in England and Scotland were often assailed and falsely charged with the errors of Cerinthus, classed with the fanatic Anabaptists and the Fifth Monarchy men. Then the outstanding English believers in the premillennial coming of Christ issued a public protest against both, the principles and conduct of this revolutionary sect.

We also find the hope of His coming among the Puritans. The great and learned author of "The Saints Everlasting

---

*Dr. Nathaniel West.

Rest," *Richard Baxter*, and many others were strong Premillennialists. Nor must we forget that the great men of New England's colonial days held the same faith of the early Church, the martyr's faith, as it has been called—the three *Mathers*, *Eliot*, *Whiting*, *Prince*, *Spaulding* of the Salem Tabernacle and many others.

Among the many great teachers in the seventeenth and eighteenth century we find *Joseph Mede*. He was born in Essex, England, in 1586 and died in 1638. Everybody of his contemporaries praised him as a pious, godly man, distinguished by his meekness, modesty and prudence. Besides this he was an acute logician, a very skillful mathematician, an able philologist having mastered many languages, and a very proficient historian. His principal work was the work of his life-time. It took up the Book of Revelation which was first published in Latin. The title was "*Clavis Apocalyptica*,"— the key to Revelation—to which was added later a larger commentary on the same book, "*In Sancti Johannis Apocalyptica Commentarius*." Both works were later published in an English translation. In his writings, as well as in many others, the future of Israel is recognized. He and other teachers, for instance Increase Mather, had found in the Scriptures the great promises which belong to Israel and gave them a literal interpretation. To illustrate this we quote Dr. Mede in an interesting comparison of Paul's conversion and the calling of the Jews. It was written by Mede in his thirty-sixth year in 1622. While not altogether correct in its details it shows how remarkably the Holy Spirit was leading towards the deeper understanding of prophecy and revealing, as stated before, the real key which unlocks the prophecies of the Old Testament.

THE MYSTERY OF PAUL'S CONVERSION: OR, THE TYPE OF THE CALLING OF THE JEWS

By Joseph Mede. 1622 A.D.

1

Paul among the sons of men the greatest zealot of the Law, and Persecutor of the way of Christ.

1

The Jews among the Nations most obstinate zealots of Moses and the most bitter enemies of the followers of Christ.

2

Paul in the height of this his zeal, and heat of his persecuting fury, found mercy and was converted.

2

The Jews, though persisting unto the last in their extremity of bitterness and mortal hate to Christians, yet will God have mercy on them, and receive them again to be His people, and be their God.

3

Paul converted by means extraordinary, and for manner strange; not, as were the rest of the Apostles, by the Ministry of any Teacher upon Earth, but by visible Revelation of Christ Jesus in His glory from Heaven; the light whereof suddenly surprising him, he heard the voice of the Lord Himself from Heaven, saying, "Saul, Saul, why persecutest thou Me "

3

The Jews not to be converted unto Christ by such means as were the rest of the Nations by the Ministry of Preachers sent unto them, but by the Revelation of Christ Jesus in His glory from Heaven, when they shall say, not, as when they saw Him in His humiliation, "Crucify Him," but, "Blessed is he that cometh in the Name of the Lord." Whose coming then shall be as a lightning out of the East, shining into the West; and the sign of the Son of Man shall appear in the clouds of Heaven, and every eye shall see Him, even of those which pierced Him, and shall lament with the spirit of grace and supplication for their so long and so shameful unbelief of their so merciful Redeemer.

4

Those who accompanied Paul at the time of this Apparition saw the light only, and were amazed; but Paul alone saw the Lord, and heard the voice which He spake unto him.

4

This Revelation of Christ from Heaven like to be most apparent to the Jews in all places where they are dispersed, but not so perhaps to the Gentiles with whom they live. The light of His Glorious Presence shall be such as the whole world shall take notice of, but those will see Him and hear His voice who pierced Him.

5

Paul no sooner converted, but was immediately inspired with the knowledge of the mysteries of Christ, without the instruction of any Apostle or Disciple; for he received not the Gospel which he preached, of man, neither was he taught it but by the Revelation of Jesus Christ. He consulteth not with the rest of the Apostles, but after fourteen years preaching, communicated to them the Gospel which he preached among the Gentiles, who added nothing unto him, but gave him the right hand of fellowship.

5

The Jews together with their miraculous calling, shall be illuminated also with the knowledge of the mysteries of the Christian faith, even as it is taught in the Reformed Churches, without any instructors from them, or conference with them; and yet when they shall communicate their faith each to other, shall find themselves to be of one communion of true belief, and give each other the right hand of fellowship.

6

Paul the last called of the Apostles.

6

The Jews to be called after all the Nations in orbe Romano, or in the circuit of the Apostle's preaching.

7

Paul once converted, the most zealous and fervent of the Apostles.

7

The Jews once converted, the most zealous and fervent of the Nations (Zech. xiii).

8

Till Paul was converted, the Gospel had small progress among the Gentiles; but when he became their Apostle, it went forward wonderfully.

8

Till the calling of the Jews, the general conversion of the Gentiles not to be expected; but the receiving Israel shall be the riches of the world, in that by their restitution the whole world shall come unto Christ.

9

The miracle of St. Paul's conversion (the person so uncapable' till then a persecutor and most bitter enemy of CHRISTIANS; the manner so wonderful as by an Apparition and Voice from Heaven), was a most powerful motive to make all those who heard and believed it, Christians; and therefore so often by St. Paul himself repeated.

9

The miracle of the Jews' conversion so much the more powerful to convert the Nations of the world not yet Christians, by how much their opposite disposition is more universally known to the world than was St. Paul's, and by how much the testimony of a whole Nation, living in so distant parts of the world, of so Divine a miracle as a Vision and Voice from Heaven, exceeds that of St. Paul, being but one man.

Mede's writings were wonderfully used and thousands had their understanding enlightened.

Joseph Mede went to be with the Lord in 1638. In the same year one was born, who became the recognized father of the Postmillennial School, still followed by many preachers and teachers of the different Protestant denominations. *Daniel Whitby* was born in Northamptonshire. He received his education in Trinity College, Oxford. He published a work, "*Treatise on the true Millennium,*" in which he advanced, what he claimed to be a, "New Discovery," opposing the premillennial coming of Christ. Boldly he declared that, "the true Millennium is not a reign of persons raised from the dead, but it is the Church flourishing gloriously for 1,000 years, after the conversion of the Jews, and the flowing in of all nations converted to Christianity." This Whitby claimed is the *first resurrection.* The whole world will be converted, followed by an undisturbed universal reign of righteousness, holiness, peace and victory. He was not an

THE REMARKABLE DEVELOPMENTS

157

"Amillennialist," denying that there ever will be a Millennium. His fatal error was the formulation of the theory that the victory of the Church in converting the whole world and establishing a reign of peace for 1,000 years, takes place *before the second coming of Christ.* The twisting he had to do, using the spiritualization and allegorization of Origen, misinterpretations of Scripture texts, misapplied quotations from the early Church fathers, we cannot follow in detail. He did what is still done in our present day school of destructive criticism, in Modernism, he ascribes the Premillennial belief to Jewish apocalyptic writings and the Sibylline oracles. This new hypothesis unscriptural throughout, unknown before, met with an astonishing success, the proof that it is not of God, for the Truth never spreads like wild-fire but error always does. Attention has been called by another why the theory of Whitby became so popular. "The terrible condition of Europe, after the French Revolution, the renewed preaching of the Gospel, resulting in great revivals, marking the eighteenth century, the new era of Missions, the foundation of Bible and Tract Societies, the interest now felt in the conversion of the world—all contributed to make Whitbyism, the postmillennial theory popular." Eminent men adopted it and joined in fighting the martyr faith, the *Maranatha* faith of the early churches. "Never in any age had it any foundation in any creed. Never, even during great spiritual revivals has it ever achieved an acceptance to be compared with that of the Premillennial faith of the early Church. While Chiliasm was, as Hase calls it, "a great Faith Article of the Apostolic Church" the Whitby Postmillennial theory has been simply the opinion of those who have accepted it as a plausible theory, easy to their comprehension. It is not the "common doctrine" of the Church, even now, and never was "doctrine" at any time. It has no countenance in any creed of the Church, in any of the Reformed symbols, least of all in the Westminster symbol."* The Whitby theory denies, what all other confessions teach on 2 Thessalonians

*Dr. Nathaniel West.

ii:8, that it means the personal advent of Christ. It teaches that the Antichrist will be destroyed by *preaching*, instead of by the second coming of Christ. Whitby showed later in life what kind of a spirit had revealed unto him his "new discovery." He became a Unitarian and denied the essential Deity of our Lord. *Such is the paternity of Postmillennialism.*

But how many scholarly witnesses rose up against this invention! How many really great men held on to the primitive faith of the blessed hope! We can mention a very few. *Sir Isaac Newton*, the discoverer of the law of gravitation, an earnest student of prophecy, declared that all the promises of glory are linked to the second advent of Christ, and that there will be set up on earth a kingdom wherein dwelleth righteousness. A namesake of Sir Isaac, *Bishop Newton* wrote, "The Kingdom of Heaven shall be established on earth. We should be cautious in making the first resurrection an allegory, least others should reduce the second to an allegory also, like those whom Paul mentioned— Hymeneus and Philetus." Dr. John Gill, the prominent Baptist Theologian spoke in words which permit no misunderstanding: "Christ will have a special, glorious and visible kingdom, in which He will reign personally on earth. This kingdom will be bound by two resurrections—first, by the resurrection of the just, at which it will begin; and, second, by the resurrection of the wicked at which it will end." Next to Joseph Mede must be placed the German scholar *Bengel*. It has been said, "his works were the first cock-crowing of that new kind of exegesis the Evangelical Church so much needed." He rejected out and out the deadly error of Augustinus that the Church and the kingdom are identical. He showed that the Revelation is a chronological prophecy. Though he made some mistakes, godly Bengel was soundly premillennial. Here is one of his choicest statements. "The events in Revelation, chapter xix, are plainly followed by those which take place, from chapter xx:11 to chapter xxii:5. The *Millennium comes in between*. He must deny the perspicuity of the Scriptures altogether, who *persists* in denying this and tries to refute it. The time will come when a pure Chiliasm (Premillennialism) will be thought an *integral part of orthodoxy*." Bengel was the instrument of the Holy Spirit in leading out a large part of the Evangelical Church in Germany into the light of the premillennial coming of our Lord. His masterwork, the Gnomen of the New Testament, is till worth while studying. Dr. Delitzsch, himself a great scholar, said the true Church owes a great debt to Bengel.

Millions still sing that blessed, that never-dying hymn, "Rock of Ages, cleft for me." The author, *Augustus Toplady*, never flinched in his faithful witness to Premillennialism. Says Toplady, "I am one of the old-fashioned people who believe the doctrine of the Millennium, and that there will be two distinct resurrections of the dead—First, of the just; and, second, of the unjust, which last resurrection of the wicked, will not be till 1000 years after the resurrection of the just." *Isaac Watts*, the author of, "Jesus shall reign, where'er the Sun, does his successive journeys run," believed as Toplady did. Count *Zinzendorf*, of the Moravian Brethren, received the truth from Bengel and he in turn led *John Wesley*, that mighty man of God and holy instrument of the Spirit of God, to become a disciple of Bengel. It has been denied, but there are the best evidences for it, Wesley was a strong Premillennialist. He preached the return of our Lord, as did his poet-brother Charles. Years ago, the writer, in reading "Tyerman on the Life and Times of Wesley," came to a paragraph in which Wesley is reported of having complimented an author by name of Thomas Hartley, who had written a book on Prophecy, Christ's coming again and on the future kingdom. Wesley endorsed it fully. We searched long, but finally obtained a copy of Hartley's book and found he taught the doctrine of Premillennialism. So every doubt as to Wesley's belief was removed. *Charles Wesley* sang it. Listen!

> "Come Lord, Thy glorious Spirit cries,
> And souls beneath the altar groan;
> Come, Lord, the Bride on earth replies,
> And perfect all our souls in one."

How often we sing in our conferences and churches another poetic outburst of John's brother:

> "Lo! He comes, with clouds descending,
>   Once for favored sinners slain;
>   Thousand, thousand saints attending,
>   Swell the triumph of His train;
>   Hallelujah! Hallelujah!
>   God appears on earth to reign.

Many of the early Methodists were scholars, godly, consecrated and believers in Christ's premillennial coming, among them Bishop Thomas Coke. *O tempora! O Mores!* Nowadays Methodism, drifting more and more into the worst kind of rationalism, denounces Premillennialism, rejects it and the beloved brethren who preach this truth are driven from pillar to post. If we are correctly informed some were deprived of their positions because they preached the hope of His coming. We could fill pages upon pages with names, illustrious names, great scholars, great preachers, godly men, who bore a faithful witness during the seventeenth and eighteenth centuries to the "Hope of His Coming." Poets too sang it, like *William Cowper*, and others. Gradually the Holy Spirit had brought the forgotten hope into prominence. Yet the "midnight cry" was yet to be sounded, the cry which arouses sleeping Christendom. The full light on prophecy and with it the midnight cry, the restoration of the primitive scriptural belief in Christ's second coming, came in the century which followed, the nineteenth century.

CHAPTER VI

The Nineteenth Century and the Full Recovery
of the Hope and Prophetic Truths

It is written, "When the enemy shall come in like a flood, the Spirit of the Lord shall lift up a standard against him" (Isa. lix:19). The powers of evil rose up like a devastating flood towards the end of the eighteenth century. The vicious *Illuminati* had issued their Abolition program, aiming at the destruction of civilization; Jacques Rousseau and other French infidel philosophers had worked towards the same end. Then came a culmination in the French Revolution with all its horrors. The mystery of Lawlessness, which Paul had seen at work already in his day, manifested its increasing power. Infidelity, God defiance filled with blasphemous hate, threatened to carry out its pit conceived plan to end Christianity and the Church. In a former volume the author expressed the opinion that the French Revolution opened the door and paved the way to the final chaotic conditions of the end of the present age, as predicted in Bible prophecy. That God-less pair, infidelity and lawlessness, stalked on through the nineteenth century, and in our own times the Church of Jesus Christ is facing an astonishing world-condition of a most striking character, a confirmation of the predictions in God's word and a harbinger of the near realization of the hope of the ages.

But the Spirit of God, in the beginning of the nineteenth century, raised a standard against it. What the Church needed was "the Lamp which shineth in a dark place" (2 Peter i:19), the lamp which gives light and never misleads, the Word of Prophecy. The Holy Spirit was pleased to restore to the true Church, that blessed hope as revealed in the Holy Scriptures, the hope of the Apostles and of the early Church. Why did He not do it before? Because the end of the age was not in sight during medieval times and the centuries which followed. The midnight cry was now to go forth, "Behold the Bridegroom cometh, go ye forth to meet Him," and as it is in the parable of the ten virgins, the

THE HOPE OF THE AGES

awakening of Christendom was to follow. Dr. West writing during the last quarter of the nineteenth century, calls attention to the wonderful progress of Premillennial doctrine adorned by a galaxy of illustrious names, by what piety, and by what unquestioned orthodoxy and scholarship it was supported! No other doctrine has come to the front of Christian thought more prominently during the nineteenth century than that of the Premillennial return of Christ. Some of the instruments used in the beginning of the nineteenth century were a company of godly, as well as scholarly men, who became the originators of what is known as the "Brethren Movement." Through them, as well as others, the truth about the Church as the body and bride of Christ, the distinctive hope of the Church, as revealed in 1 Thessalonians iv:16-18, His imminent coming for His saints, the hope of Israel, their final great tribulation, the restoration of the Roman Empire in its final form, the meaning of the final Antichrist, as well as the political head of the Roman empire, the little horn of Daniel's prophecy, and many other phases of the premillennial coming of our Lord, now familiar to all painstaking students of the Bible, were brought to light by these godly men. We mention a few of their names: Dr. Edward Cronin, Lord Congleton, A. N. Groves, William J. Stokes, J. G. Bellett, William Kelly, Benjamin W. Newton, Samuel P. Tregelles, George Müller, the great man of prayer, and especially John Nelson Darby. The latter translated the entire Bible into English, German and French, and was greatly used in shedding light on prophecy. To these names many others could be added, Dr. Neatby, Dr. Baedeker, Deck, Sir Robert Anderson, a counsellor of the late Queen Victoria, F. W. Grant, and many others. Unfortunately some of these men, mighty in the Scriptures, who had given such a splendid testimony to the unity of the body of Christ, created new, and often, bitter divisions. Nevertheless they were much used, and hundreds of preachers and teachers have acknowledged the great debt they owe to these servants of the Lord Jesus Christ.

With the nineteenth century the belief which dominated

the Reformation period, that the Papacy is the Antichrist, disappeared almost entirely, though still held by a certain school of interpretation. When Napoleon the First arose in his power, when he revealed his ambitions to be crowned Emperor of the Roman Empire, when he wanted to call a Jewish Sanhedrin to accomplish the coronation in Jerusalem, many thought he must be the predicted Antichrist; some even acclaimed him the man of sin, but they were found false prophets. Such hasty assertions of men, who instead of interpreting prophecy, attempted to prophesy themselves, were made again and again in connection with day-setting, when Christ would come, in spite of the fact that our Lord stated that neither day nor hour were known. It always ended, and always will end, in failure, yet the "day setting fanaticism" continues. One Michael Baxter of London, a good man but misguided, published a volume under the title of "The Forty Coming Wonders." He had everything figured out; he gave the date for the rapture of the Church, the rise of the little horn, the time when Christ would reappear and when the Millennium would begin. When the dates had expired and nothing happened, he confessed his mistake and printed another edition setting the dates ahead, only to find it was another mistake, yet he seemed to keep at it till the day of his death. Another notable fanatic was William Miller, who was born in Pittsfield, Mass. Like others before and after him he juggled the 2,300 days in Daniel viii:14, claiming that they were years. To his own satisfaction he had discovered the exact day in which in 1843 the Lord would appear in the clouds of heaven. Many people believed him, gave up their various occupations, prepared white robes in which they expected to ascend.

Then came the Adventist movement. Seventh Day Adventism holds many perverse beliefs, such as soul-sleep, the annihilation of the wicked, and other errors, and much they teach about the return of Christ is not founded on Scripture. Still another mis-leader was the founder of a system, in which a number of heresies, which sprang up in post-Apostolic days were revived. The founder was one self-styled, "Pastor Russell." His system assumed various names; Millennial Dawnism, Watchtower, People's Pulpit; Bible Student Association, etc., etc. At the present time some call themselves "Jehovah's Witnesses." Russell invented a theory in which he taught that Christ returned in 1874 in a secret way, and that forty years later He would be manifested publicly and therefore the Millennium would begin in 1914. But instead of the Millennium the world war started in that year. After this ignominious failure other dates were selected which all turned out to be hallucinations. The system is really Unitarian as it denies the essential Godhood of our Lord. This does not by any means exhaust the list of other spurious movements. We pass them by besides many individuals, some undoubtedly mentally unbalanced, who predicted one thing after another. We shall later mention the "Pentecostal Movement," which in many respects is kin to the Montanism of the second century.

But why mention these erratic movements which claim to teach the Premillennial coming, who teach much truth connected with it, but have, at the same time fallen for the most soul-destroying errors? We give two reasons. It is a demonstration that the same perverting, corrupting and counterfeiting power, which was at work in the beginning of the church by fostering a carnal Chiliasm, by linking with it contorted and false doctrines, is still at work. That power knows the true, scriptural doctrine of Premillennialism; more than that the head of that power, Satan, hates the true doctrine and has been doing all he can to keep man from believing it, and that for his own sinister purposes. To bring it in disrepute, make it obnoxious and in this way to blind eyes and keep Christians away from seeing, accepting and living that hope, which is one of the most powerful incentives to holy living, self-sacrificial service, and which carries with it untold blessings, comfort, peace and joy, is Satan's purpose.

The other reason is the perversion of the doctrine of our Lord's return, and the errors which have been associated with it, are used against those who teach the Premillennial coming in a sane, scriptural and spiritual way. The author answered some seventeen years ago a certain Postmillennial writer, who mentioned, besides ourself the following brethren of fragrant memory—R. A. Torrey, I. M. Haldeman, James M. Gray, C. I. Scofield and others, and then added that they in their Premillennialism are with Seventh Day Adventism, Russellism, Dowieism of the same family. How often the author in his long ministry, preaching the Gospel and teaching the hope of His coming, has been warned against as being "a Russellite," or a follower of similar sects of error and delusion. In the same manner they accused the disciple of Polycarp, Irenaeus, in the second century, as well as others.

But we must now mention some of the great witnesses for the Premillennial hope who were raised up during the past nineteenth century. One of the great preachers, teacher and outstanding scholar during the past century was the famous theologian of Scotland, *Dr. Thomas Chalmers*. He was a strong Premillennialist. In his "Sabbath Readings" we find the following paragraph: "I desire to cherish a more habitual and practical faith than heretofore in that coming which even the first Christians were called to hope for with all earnestness, even though many centuries were to elapse ere the hope could be realized; and how much more we, who are so much nearer this great fulfilment than at the time they believed." And again, even stronger, "Of this I am satisfied, that the next coming of Christ will be a coming, not to final judgment but a coming *to usher in the millennium*. I utterly despair of the universal prevalence of Christianity as the result of a missionary process. I look for its conclusive establishment through a widening passage of desolations and judgments, with the demolition of our civil and ecclesiastical structures. Overturn, overturn, overturn is the watchword of our approaching Lord." At the same time lived *Edward Irving*, befriended by Dr. Chalmers. Edward Irving was a brilliant preacher who attracted thousands. But he was of an erratic spirit. He preached the coming of Christ, and its nearness. All went well till one day there appeared in the midst of his congregation,

what was claimed to be a restoration of "the gift of tongues."
Members of the congregation began to prophesy. It was all
traced to the subtle influence of demons. Once more demon
power brought reproach upon the hope of Christ's coming.*
Edward Irving himself taught evil doctrines and was expelled
from the Kirk. Like Montanus he claimed a restoration of
apostolic gifts and super-manifestations of the Holy Spirit.

Witnesses of Christ's return, who rejected the unscriptural, traditional belief, that His return would bring a
universal resurrection, a universal judgment and the end
of the Kosmos, who taught and preached the faith and hope
of the early Church, arose everywhere. While it is true
that in Germany much of the destructive criticism had its
origin and the rationalism of the Tübingen School sowed its
evil seed, it must not be overlooked that in Germany mighty
men of God, godly and scholarly, defended the evangelical
faith and at the same time stood up for the premillennial
faith and hope. They left many commentaries which
proved a most effectual testimony against rationalism and
at the same time brought a remarkable revival of prophetic
study and a widespread acceptance of the premilliennal hope
throughout the evangelical Church. We mention some of
these great German expositors, Auberlen, Baumgarten,
Blumhardt, Krumacher, Starke, Stier, Luthard, Christlieb,
Koch, Stockmayer, Lechler, Lange, Rothe, Olshausen,
Gerlach, Dorner, Hebart and scores of others. In the
Netherlands we find such men of undoubted scholarship,
great leaders of religious thought, as, DaCosta, Capadose,
Roorda and Van Oosterzee. Still more numerous are the
men of Great Britain who in the nineteenth century heralded
the martyr faith, the martyr hope, the hope of the apostolic
fathers, the hope so solidly grounded in the Word of God.
In Scotland besides Dr. Chalmers we find Horatius and
Andrew Bonar, great preachers, theologians, consecrated
pastors, soul-winners and gifted poets. In vain do we look
today among the "Amillennialists," and the Postmillen-

*See Sir Robert Anderson on *Spirit Manifestation*.

nialists, for men of their calibre. Those who attack and belittle "that blessed hope" are mere dwarfs in comparison with those giants of thought, scholarship and piety. McCheyne, whose early death was lamented by thousands, belonged to the same noble company, including Mackay, Stewart, Cummings, Frazer, Anderson and many, many more. Nor do we forget Jamieson and Faussett, who jointly produced a reliable premillennial commentary, which is still in circulation. Charles H. Spurgeon preached the hope of His coming to thousands in his Metropolitan Tabernacle. We must also mention the able commentator, the Hebrew Christian, Dr. Adolph Saphir.

In the Church of England we find Bishops, Deans, Canons, Rectors, who earnestly preached prophetic truths. We mention a few: Bishop Ryle of Liverpool; Webb-Peploe, Girdlestone, Horne, Bickersteth, Melville, Rainsford, Alford and scores of others. Even more numerous are the premillennial preachers and teachers, living during the nineteenth century in the United States. We could fill several pages with their names, some forgotten on earth, but recorded in heaven. Professor Duffield of Princeton, Cuthbert Hall of Union Theological Seminary, before it had plunged into the quicksands of modernism, Joel Parker, S. H. Kellogg, Professor Morehead of the United Presbyterian Church, A. J. Gordon, James H. Brookes, Professor Stifler of Crozier, W. J. and Albert Erdman, George and Thomas Needham, Pitzer, Dinwiddie, Marvin, L. W. Munhall, Durbin, Foster, Dr. Seiss of the Lutheran Church, Jacobs, the two Dr. Tyngs of the Protestant Episcopal Church, Patterson, Dr. Schaff, also of Union Theological Seminary and hundreds more. Recently we came across a long autographed letter, addressed to us in 1894 by aged William Nast. Dr. Nast was the father of German Methodism. Once a liberalist, but converted he became a splendid witness for the truth of the Gospel and for the blessed hope. He encouraged the writer, then a young man, to persevere in his premillennial testimony.

It was in the eighties of the nineteenth century when a

company of preachers and educators gathered in Bible Conferences for the study of the Word of God and especially prophecy. The gathering became known as "the Niagara Bible Conference," because it convened mostly at Niagara on the Lake. We give the names of some of the speakers: James H. Brookes, H. B. Parsons, Professor Morehead, Arthur T. Pierson, a brilliant speaker and scholar, W. J. and Albert Erdman, George C. Needham, C. I. Scofield, Dr. Nathaniel West, Marvin, Major Whittle, Bishop Nicholson, Henry Foster, Canon Howitt and the author of this volume. All are now with the Lord with the exception of Canon Howitt and the author. This conference exerted a wide influence. "*The Truth*," edited by Dr. James H. Brookes, a prince among expositors, gave reports of the different sessions and in this way premillennial truths were spread over our land. When Dr. Brookes was called home his testimony had ended. But it pleased God to use *Our Hope* founded by the author in 1894, and still edited by him, in the continuation of the testimony of the blessed hope.

We must mention another fact. Great movements were started during the nineteenth century. Foreign Mission enterprises, such as the China Inland Mission, African Missions and others were launched. Great interest was also created in giving the Gospel to the Jewish people everywhere, societies for the evangelization of the Jews were founded in England, Germany, and the United States. Great revivals took place, not spurious, but the genuine work of the Holy Spirit, by which many thousands were saved. Interest in Bible Study was deepened and we witnessed also the foundation of Bible Institutes. How did these spiritual movements come to pass? Did they originate through the advocates of liberalism? Did the Tübingen-Straus-Baur School send forth missionaries into foreign lands? Did a stiff, ritualistic, lifeless Protestantism bring about revivals and an interest in Bible Study? These questions must be answered negatively. The astonishing revival of the faith and hope of the early Church, the hope of His coming, the midnight-cry which was heard in the beginning of the century, and was increasingly heralded, the restoration of the "forgotten hope," the glorious vision of the re-appearing of our Lord and Saviour Jesus Christ to establish His kingdom, backed by the signs of the times, produced through the energy of the Holy Spirit these spiritual movements. Premillennialism kept step with missionary efforts, to bring the Gospel as quickly as possible to every nation so that the elect number of the body of Christ might be called out. The missionaries who went forth to China, India, Japan, Africa and the islands of the sea were overwhelmingly Premillennialists. The Coming of the Lord was one of the incentives to render self-sacrificial service. The leading Evangelists towards the end of the nineteenth century, Moody and Sankey, and many others were Premillennialists. Most of the Bible expositors, who furnished the household of faith with "meat in due season," were not the servants who say "my Lord delayeth His coming," but those who had seen in the Bible the vision of His coming. The wise virgins arose everywhere to trim their lamps to go forth to meet the Bridegroom, and while waiting, they were far from being, as their enemies branded them, "star-gazers." They served as only those can serve who truly "wait for His Son from heaven."

CHAPTER VII

Our Own Times

The Whitbyan Postmillennial theory is a form of evolution, call it religious or ecclesiastical. But the law of evolution, any kind of evolution, if there is no progress, is disproved and if so should be abandoned. The author has traced in another volume* the world events covering the history of the twentieth century up to the year 1936. What a terrible slump has taken place in the first three decades of the boasted twentieth century civilization! What horrible things have taken place! A world war was fought by so-called "Christian nations," supported by heathen nations, the most disastrous war in all history. A revolution in Russia, in comparison with which the French Revolution pales into insignificance. Several million human beings were cruelly murdered to make possible the establishment of Sovietism, ruled by a band of murderers. Atheism and Antichristianity is rising everywhere. Crime is rampant the world over. Nations have armed and are still arming for a gigantic conflict which no mind can imagine and no pen can describe. Every form of lawful government is not only threatened, but is nearing a complete collapse, this includes our own American democracy. Dictators control Europe today. Mussolini marches onward in his ambitious endeavor to have another Roman World Empire; Hitler, the modern Haman, persecutes the Jews, and reaches out towards the East, dreaming of a Germanic control which is to extend from the Rhine to the shores of the Black Sea. The United States are in the throes of political corruption, a planned misrule, which must eventually lead to bankruptcy followed probably by a civil war which may outdo anything in previous history. Morally the world sinks lower and lower. Christendom is turning more and more away from the supernatural, the foundation of true Christianity, turning from the spiritual to the material, giving up the message of power

*"Hopeless—Yet There is Hope."

for social improvements. Leaders become advocates of Atheistic Communism. A clique has arisen in the land of Luther which aims at the destruction of the Church and Christianity. The faith as revealed in God's infallible Book is abandoned; apostasy is seen everywhere. World conversion, the world accepting Christianity? *What mockery!* The nations of the world were never as far away from accepting Christ as Saviour and recognize Him as Lord as in 1938. And if we should write 1939-1940, etc., each year will be marked by worse conditions.

Where is the *"Gospel leaven"* which Whitbyan Postmillennialism proclaims, which leavens everything? Is the Church on the high-road to conquer, establish righteousness and peace as the foundation of "the Millennium," or is the professing Church the victim of Delilah which has shorn it of its power? Only one who shuts his eyes deliberately to existing conditions can maintain the unscriptural, as well as unreasonable, belief that our age is rapidly improving and nearing a consummation of righteousness. Apart from the teachings of the Word of God, the chaotic world-conditions, the gathering clouds, indicating greater tempests and devastating powers, answer the Whitbyan theory of a Millennium of righteousness and peace, set up by the Church.

World conditions as they are today are a confirmation of Bible prophecy. Look at it! The predicted events, to take place when, not the world comes to an end, but when the present age, the times of the Gentiles close, are looming up larger and larger on the horizon of our solemn times. The stage is preparing and being set for the last act of the drama of our age, controlled by the forces of evil under the leadership of the god of this age, the prince of this age, Satan. The final conflict between the seed of the woman and the seed of the serpent, ending victoriously for the seed of the woman, for Christ and His Body, the true Church, is at hand. How the destructive forces are massing! Against God and against His Christ, against every government which maintains principles of righteousness, against all civilized humanity cherishes! The mystery of lawlessness is nearing its climax. It will bring the manifestation of the man of sin, the son of perdition, who claims to be God taking his place in the temple of God, showing himself, by lying signs and wonders that he is God, to deceive and to corrupt. It has become evident that the Reformation belief, that the Papacy is this masterpiece of Satan, is no longer tenable. No Pope ever claimed to be God. Popes are the spurious Vice-regents of Christ, none ever said, "I am Christ." The abomination of desolation (Matt. xxiv:15) is not connected with the Church, but is connected with Israel's land. Start- ling has been the rapid advance of Zionism among the Jews. The World War made possible its program. Palestine under British mandate has been transformed, colonies flourish. Never before in the history of the times of the Gentiles could Palestine boast of 400,000 Jewish inhabitants. A restora- tion is taking place, but God is left out. It is an attempt to solve the "Jewish Question," apart from God's oath bound covenants, apart from Him, who is Israel's Messiah. All will end in that predicted "great tribulation," for the Jews first and also for the Gentiles, but not for the Church of God. Then will appear the dictatorship of the pit. These prophecies which a generation ago appeared misty, stand out now in bold relief, Jewish ambitions and conditions shed a remarkable light on prophecies relating to the end of the age. The prophecies of Paul, Peter, John James and Jude as to the moral and religious conditions of "the last days" of our age are with us. Modernism has dragged the Lord Jesus Christ from the throne of His Saviourhood and His Lordship and degraded Him to the level of a religious leader, a philoso- pher, a great teacher and example, who only lives by the words He spoke, denied as existent in His glorified personal- ity at the right hand of God.

With such signs of the times increasing year after year since the beginning of the twentieth century, there was bound to come a great revival in the study of Prophecy, a revival in true, scriptural and sane Premillennialism, the faith and hope of the Church of Jesus Christ in the begin- ning. And so it has been and so it is still. The midnight

cry had been sounded; the wise virgins flock together. A
new impetus was given to the study of Prophecy. Thousands
received the light. The Whitbyan "bats" are still dashing
about aimlessly as ever and Modernism, so closely related
to Postmillennialism, is still trying to bring about a better
world, not by the Gospel, but by political schemes and a
united front of Catholics, Protestants (?) and Jews.

As we pointed out in our previous chapter the restored
hope, the primitive hope of the Church, produced during
the nineteenth century the great spiritual movements,
foreign missionary activities, revivals, a deepened interest
in the study of the Holy Scriptures and other blessed results.
This is true, even in a higher degree, in the present century.
The men used in evangelistic labors, bringing the true Gospel
of Grace to hundreds of thousands, with a fruitage which
cannot be measured by numbers, were and are all Premillennialists, who did not hesitate to give witness to the
blessed hope. We mention a few—Reuben A. Torrey, J.
Wilbur Chapman, William Sunday, and scores of others.
If we were to mention now the brethren who are active
throughout the English speaking world, as well as in other
countries, Germany, Holland, Switzerland, the Scandinavian
countries and others, in Bible teaching, Christian education and missionary efforts, we would have to fill a
dozen pages with their names and all of them are staunch
believers in the coming of the Lord and in His coming
kingdom on earth. They are found in all evangelical
denominations. Many have been called home to rest
from their labors, to join the waiting Church up yonder.
We mention a few—W. H. Griffith Thomas, I. M. Haldeman, A. C. Dixon, C. I. Scofield, D. M. Stearns, Canon
Dyson Hague, Elmore Harris, Canon Waite, Ford C.
Ottman, John F. Carson, Arthur T. Pierson, Walter Scott,
Samuel Ridout, Leon Tucker, James M. Gray, Charles A.
Blanchard, L. W. Munhall, and many more. We cannot
begin to give even a small number of the names of those who
carry on Bible teaching work from coast to coast, who feed the
flock of God; nearly all of them, with very few exceptions,

are sound Premillennialists. Bible Conferences, monthly
meetings, interdenominational and undenominational gather-
ings for Bible study multiplied during the last thirty years.
Two outstanding prophetic conferences were held under
peculiar providential circumstances. It was in the fall of 1913
when the suggestion came to the writer to send out a call for a
Prophetic Conference to be held in the spring of the year
1914. It was done in cooperation with Dr. James M. Gray
and the Moody Bible Institute in Chicago. None knew that
the World War would start in that year. Thousands
gathered from everywhere, great blessing followed, the testimony was greatly honored by God. A similar conference,
though on a smaller scale, was held in 1916 in Philadelphia.
It was in the spring of 1918 when a hundred New York State
preachers, educators and business men, under the leadership of the writer sent out a call for a Prophetic Conference
to be held in New York City during November of that year.
Nobody knew that on November the eleventh an armistice
would be signed. God knew and made possible a most remarkable testimony for our Lord and His return and coming
kingdom. Carnegie Hall, seating over 5,000, was filled night
after night, and overflow meetings had to be held. The
prophetic testimony was given in great power and was felt
from coast to coast. Since the publication of *Our Hope*
as a prophetic Monthly in 1894, scores of similar periodicals
have made their appearance spreading the true teachings
of the second advent, teaching the true Biblical eschatology.
The men who write Bible expositions, Bible annotations,
who are the authors of faith-building, literature, whose
written messages feed God's people everywhere, are almost
entirely Premillennialists. The sound educational institutions, which stand for the faith once and for all delivered
unto the Saints, are in charge of Premillennial educators.
We mention the Theological Seminary of Dallas, Texas;
Wheaton College; the Stony Brook School for Boys and the
many Bible Institutes, besides the Moody Institute, the
Northwestern Bible Training College, in Minneapolis, the
Philadelphia School of the Bible and similar institutes in

New York, New Orleans, Washington, Portland, Oregon; Providence, Rhode Island; Los Angeles, California; Baltimore, Maryland; and in other cities. What activities! What consecration! What dissemination of Bible knowledge!

Read denominational church papers and you find the complaint of empty churches. In many places a Lord's Day evening service is out of the question. The automobile and the golf course have made such services impossible in many places. Weekly prayer meetings are no longer held. But there are churches filled to overflowing and prayer meetings are attended by hundreds. The preachers are true to the divine commission and preach the Word. They follow the Spirit's exhortation, "These things speak, and exhort, and rebuke with all authority" (Titus ii:15). And "these things" include, as the context shows, "that blessed hope, and the glorious appearing of the great God and our Saviour Jesus Christ." Not scores, but hundreds of faithful servants of Christ, pastors in different denominations preach in a scriptural way the hope of His coming, they do not neglect prophecy, nor do they magnify it at the expense of other vital doctrines. Their church buildings are filled. They are soul winners; under their ministry hundreds of believers are built up in their most holy faith; there is likewise great consecrated liberality in the support of missions and all the blessed by-products of true Christianity. By their fruits ye shall know them. God's mighty seal of approval rests upon those who do not rob the Lord Jesus Christ of the glory which belongs to Him, who preach faithfully His return, when He shall receive "glory and dominion for ever and ever."

Yet in spite of these facts, which are apparent and cannot be denied, Anti-Millennialists, the followers of the Whitbyan Postmillennial invention, Modernists, Evolutionists, Amillennialists, continue to point their fingers at the zealous witnesses of His return and say, "He is a good man, able and a splendid Christian, but he is a Premillennialist." They rake up the fanaticism, so often displayed in the past, and identify it with the true Scriptural faith taught by the

prophets, by our Lord and the Apostles, as to His coming
and His kingdom. The fanaticism of the Jewish conception,
attempting by fire and sword to set up an earthly kingdom,
denying also that Jesus is the Messiah; the still greater carnal
fanaticism of the Anabaptists, who claimed to believe in
Christ, under Satanic delusion trying to set up a kingdom by
fire and sword, before Christ's return, the movement of
the Fifth Monarchy men, are all as different from the Spirit
revealed Premillennial doctrine as day is from night. One
would expect at least that seminary trained men, students
of Systematic Theology and Church History would recognize this difference. Yet they hold on to traditional beliefs,
fall back on the Augsburg or Westminster confessions and
standards, though neither of them rejects the scriptural
premillennial faith.

As it was in the first centuries and in the centuries which
followed, so it is in our own times, during the twentieth
century, all kinds of heresies, delusions, hallucinations and
various forms of fanaticism are linked through the wiles of
the devil with the Bible doctrine of Christ's return. All these
counterfeits and perversions have but one purpose to serve,
to make the great hope, Christ's coming glory, as obnoxious
as possible and destroy the faith in that hope.

We mention a few of these delusions which the devil has
brought to the front in recent times. In the beginning of our
century a man flourished who claimed to be "Elijah, the
restorer," Alexander Dowie. He founded on the shores of
Lake Michigan a town, which he named "Zion City." It
was one of the most foolish attempts to bring about the fulfilment of God's promises to the true and only Zion in
Palestine in the State of Illinois. The spurious Elijah who
had much to say about prophecy went into bankruptcy.

It was in 1904 when in a small meeting of excited colored
people in Los Angeles, California, something was started in
religious frenzy which soon spread in every direction, from
country to country and continent to continent. It was
claimed that another "Day of Pentecost" had come, evidenced by the restored gift of tongues. It spread like wild

fire. In this respect it resembled the Spiritistic Movement of the middle of the nineteenth century which spread everywhere, indicating the sinister influences behind it. As a result of that California meeting the so-called "Pentecostal Movement" originated, as well as several others which use the word "Apostolic." These movements are almost a reproduction of the Montanism of the second century. Like Montanism the Pentecostal sects claim a continuation of the sign gifts of a miraculous nature. They claim a fulfilment of Joel ii:28-29, without considering the context. They teach that each Christian must experience an individual Pentecost, and that its evidence is "talking in tongues." Connected with it, as it was in Montanism, are trances, foamings at the mouth and finally a conglomeration of sounds, bellowings and jerky words, which are claimed to be a supernatural gift. But no one seems to have been able to interpret these tongues. They also claim miraculous healings and numerous of these fanatics, to prove the sign "they shall take up serpents," permitted themselves to be bitten by rattlesnakes; some recovered, others died as the result of their presumption. We never heard of one, however, who drank a dose of arsenic to prove Mark xvi:18. As it was in Montanism women leadership is prominent in Pentecostalism. One of the outstanding ones is the widely known Aime Semple McPherson. She and others talk about the return of the Lord, claim to have had vision about it, lying visions of course. Evidently the same power, which produced Montanism has brought it back in the form of Pentecostalism to hinder and hurt the true faith of His return. Seventh Day Adventism, with its evil doctrines, Millennial Dawnism, "Jehovah's witnesses," Pentecostalism, Dowieism, Christadelphians, and other erratic cults, not to forget Mormonism, all have something to say about Christ's second coming. Dates are set for His appearing; figures are juggled to prove these dates; certain persons are picked out as being the Antichrist. During the war it was Kaiser William II. Now it is either Mussolini or Hitler. With all these fanatical, erratic and unscriptural delusions the true believer in the Biblical doctrine of His

return *has no sympathy whatever*. More than that, true Premillennial teachers warn against these cults and their soul
destroying errors.

We must not forget another theory which originated in
the nineteenth century and which is still upheld by many
in the entire English speaking world. It is Anglo-Israelism.
It teaches that the supposedly lost ten tribes of Israel are
the English and American people, in spite of the well-proved
fact that both nations are an amalgamation, a melting pot,
of many nations. They too speak of the coming of the Lord
and of His earthly kingdom. Some of these delusionists
declared that the erstwhile Prince of Wales, now known as
the Duke of Windsor, would assume in being crowned King
of England, the name of David, and that during his reign
Christ would come and that he would hand over the British
Empire to Him. No need to tell our readers what became
of this delusion.

The survival of the Scripture Doctrine of His Coming and
His kingdom is next to miraculous and an evidence that it
is truth and not fable. "When we consider, for but one
moment, against what fearful odds this precious doctrine
of the personal appearing of the Incarnate Redeemer on
earth, to unite the heirs and the inheritance in a glorious
visible kingdom, has had to force its way through the centuries, we stand amazed, and confess that only because it
is an imperishable truth of God has it been able to survive
the ordeal through which it has passed." It is victorious in
the twentieth century. It is the great light-house sending its
guiding rays across the stormy sea of nations, with its ever
rising turbulent waves guiding to a heaven of rest, a haven of
peace and glory. It is the most needed message for our
times, which keeps the lamps of Christian testimony burning
not in a sickly flicker, but with increasing brightness. It is
the truth needed to uphold in these days of confusion and
distress, the truth which cheers, for in the stormy night we
still hear the voice of the coming One, as the toiling disciples
on the Galilean Sea heard it—"Be not afraid! It is I!" It
is the truth which best of all, keeps Himself before our hearts

and through the energy of the indwelling Spirit creates that blessed longing to meet Him face to face. It is the safeguard keeping believers from error, from worldliness and from the blasting indifference of our times.

Perhaps as never before there arises from so many hearts the God-given prayer, as it does now, "Even so, Come, Lord Jesus." Louder and louder this prayer is heard, from the lips of suffering Chinese believers, from the prison camps in Siberia, from harassed believers in Spain, from the noble confessors in Germany, from every country and from every nation. We visit hospitals and from the couches of pain, from the lips of the hopeless incurable comes the same prayer. And thousands of believers, even those who are prosperous in earthly things, are becoming sick of this restless age with its approaching collapse and are homesick for that city above which hath foundations, whose builder and maker is God (Heb. xi:10), the Father's House, the heavenly Jerusalem. On account of world conditions an inner consciousness has been created in thousands of hearts the conviction that the time of His coming cannot be far away, that it must be near at hand. "The night is far spent, the day is at hand." And well may we say the star of that blessed hope shone never as bright as now. Thousands of hearts look for the rising of the Morningstar, His Coming for His Saints. And the Spirit and the Bride say, Come!

CHAPTER VIII

The Approaching Realization

The heavens and the earth are in a waiting attitude. We look up and we see our blessed Lord Himself waiting and expecting. Once He waited as the Only Begotten in the bosom of the Father for the appointed time, the hour fixed before the foundation of the world, to clothe Himself with a human body, to appear among men in the form of a servant. But now He is waiting as the First-begotten from among the dead for another appointed time, when once more He will come forth from the third heaven to manifest His glory, and to execute God's redemption purposes, culminating in His enthronement as King of kings and Lord of lords, when all things are put under His feet. When will it be? "But of that day and that hour knoweth no man, no, not the angels which are in heaven, neither the Son, but the Father" (Mark xiii:32). In His Godhood our Lord certainly knows all the purposes of God, but in the quoted passage He speaks as the Son of Man; in all His redemption work past, present and future, He is subject to the Father's will. Let us also remind ourselves of the way He answered the last question of His disciples. They had asked Him: "Wilt Thou at this time restore again the kingdom to Israel?" He answered: "It is not for you to know the times or the seasons which the Father has put in His own power" (Acts i:6, 7). But before He comes back to earth again in power and great glory to claim His crown rights over the earth, God's purpose in the present age must be finished. That purpose is not, as stated before, that all nations be converted and brought into the imagined "church-kingdom." God's purpose is that during this age the body of Christ, the Church, be gathered from among Jews and Gentiles. This is the great work of the Holy Spirit beginning at Pentecost, when all assembled believers were baptized into one body, when the Church came into existence, till some day the last member of that elect body is joined and the body is complete. Then He will arise from His mediatorial place as the Priest and Advocate of His people to receive unto Himself "His many sons," to bring them unto glory (Heb. ii:10), to be with Him joint-heirs of that glory which the Father has given Him. This will mean the fulfilment of that great and precious revelation penned by the Apostle Paul in First Thessalonians iv:16-18. That great reception will take place not on earth, but the righteous dead raised, with the living believers on earth will be caught up together "to meet the Lord in the air." What a meeting that will be! From that meeting place He will lead the redeemed hosts upward through the glorious portals of the third heaven into the Father's house with its many mansions.

Nor is He waiting alone. There are multitudes of the redeemed also patiently waiting with Him. They are the disembodied spirits of the righteous of all ages. The Old Testament and New Testament believers. They are an ever increasing waiting company in the presence of the Lord. It has not pleased God to give us full information as to their condition, save that we know they are at rest. Nor do we know the glories of Paradise. Often the question is asked, "Do they know what is going on here on earth?" We do not know. But we know they are waiting to be participants in the first resurrection, not a spiritual resurrection, but a resurrection of their bodies. How they must wait for that momentous event when Christ arises from the Father's throne, to give the commanding shout which will result in the realization of their hope. They are waiting thus to be made perfect. The martyrs of Old Testament times are in that waiting company. We read of them in Hebrews ii:32-40. The still greater number of New Testament martyrs, beginning with the first martyr, Stephen, the hundreds of thousands of martyrs who suffered a cruel death during the Roman pagan persecutions are all waiting. So are the hosts of martyrs no man can number, who died under the vicious regime of Papal Rome and the recent martyrs of the most terrible revolution of all history, the Russian revolution, when millions suffered martyrdom through fire, sword, scourgings, tortures, famines and pestilences. What a waiting multitude, waiting for the fulness of glory, waiting for their rewards, waiting for the crowning day, waiting for the manifestation of the sons of God!

How little we know of that great world above us, the world of angels. They are closely linked with the story of redemption in the past. Throughout this age when man is to "walk by faith and not by sight," they are no longer visible, though we know "they are ministering spirits, sent forth to minister for them who shall be heirs of salvation." But when the hour comes, the hour of His glorious manifestation, the hour of His triumph, the hour when every eye shall see Him, angels will have a large share in it all. It is written that angels will be with Him, "when the Lord Jesus shall be revealed from heaven with His mighty angels" (2 Thess. i:7). He will use them as executors of His judgments. The reapers at the time of the harvest, the end of our age, will be angels. "The Son of man shall send forth His angels, and they shall gather out of His kingdom all things that offend, and them which do iniquity" (Matt. xiii:39, 40). They will be used to bring together the scattered nation Israel—"He shall send His angels with a great sound of a trumpet, and they shall gather together His elect from the four winds, from one end of heaven to the other" (Matt. xxiv:31). They will be visibly present throughout His kingdom reign, for our Lord tells us, "Ye shall see heaven open, and the angels of God ascending and descending upon the Son of man" (John. i:51). For all this they are waiting. What mighty Hallelujahs will burst forth some day when the door of the third heaven swings open wide, when He comes forth to receive His co-heirs and when finally the triumphal march begins and the angels of God shall fall in line!

Other beings are waiting in the heavenlies. Scripture tells us that there are "wicked spirits in the heavenly places" (Ephes. vi:12, correct rendering). The heaven surrounding our earth is the seat of the kingdom of darkness over which Satan is the head. That is the reason why one of his names is "the prince of the power of the air" (Ephes. ii:2). From the air he reaches down into our sphere and acts as "the god of this age." He and the world of fallen angels and demons are waiting. The devil knows from Scripture more than many an unbelieving theological professor knows concerning the future. He knows there is coming a mighty battle, which will have to be fought "in the air." There will be war in heaven. Michael, that mighty Archangel, mentioned frequently in connection with the end history of our age, will summon his angels. The dragon with his evil hosts will have to face him. The time of Satan's defeat is at hand. "And the great dragon was cast out, that old serpent, called the Devil, and Satan, which deceiveth the whole world; he was cast out into the earth, and his angels were cast out with him" (Rev. xii:7-12). And when he is cast out he will turn his vicious wrath, his great wrath against those who live on earth, for we read, "Woe to the inhabiters of the earth and of the sea! for the devil is come down to you, having great wrath, because he knoweth that he hath but a short time." He will institute the great tribulation. The Church of Jesus Christ, not Christendom, but the true Church, His body and His Bride, will not be on earth, for true believers are delivered from this satanic wrath to come.

And what waiting there is upon earth. His true Church as never before, since apostolic days is waiting "for His Son from heaven." As we have shown that blessed hope has been restored by the Holy Spirit; true scriptural knowledge concerning it has been increased everywhere. Erstwhile heathen in China, Japan, Africa and elsewhere, saved by grace, know that hope and with millions of other believers in every continent rejoice in the prospects of glory and pray, "Even so, Come Lord Jesus." Sighs and groans arise from hundreds of thousands of hearts longing for the promised redemption. That part of Christendom which rejects the faith, once and for all delivered unto the saints, is also waiting. Their hopes of evolution of a better world will miscarry. When finally our Lord reappears the delusive hopes of apostate Christendom will be forever ended. No more "Postmillennialism," the Whitbyan invention, and no more "Amillennialism," another invention, that there will be no personal Kingdom reign of Christ over the earth, after Christ's return.

The nations are waiting. Did our infallible Lord announce for the nations during this present age, when He is absent in Person, a program of peace? Did He indicate that, as this age draws to its close, all nations would be united into a "Universal Brotherhood," that Nationalism would disappear entirely, that all distinctions would be wiped out and after a successful propaganda against war and armaments, a warless world is to follow and the miseries of human existence will speedily disappear? Such are the dreams of men who reject God's revelation. Our Lord did not predict such things. Wars and rumors of wars; nation rising against nation and kingdom against kingdom to the very end of the age! Helpless and hopeless is being written larger and larger across the political horizon of our times. "Vain is the help of man." The nations, though they are ignorant of it, are waiting for One who will not only speak peace, but who has the power to give peace on earth, our coming Lord.

The condition of the Jews is equally hopeless. The dream of Theodore Herzl, the father of political Zionism, recently so rosy, on account of an astonishing restoration of the promised land, has been greatly disturbed. The immediate future of Zionism in Palestine is very dark. Antisemitism increases everywhere. What are they going to do? Alas! that they still refuse to believe that Christ is "the Hope of Israel." Yet He, and only He, is their salvation. Some day a believing remnant among them will pray as Asaph, the saint of old, prayed, "Let Thy hand be upon the Man of Thy right hand, upon the Son of man, whom Thou madest strong for Thyself" (Psa. lxxx:17).

How long will this waiting last? World conditions give us an answer. Never before in the history of our age have the predictions of the Bible so positively been confirmed as they are in our twentieth century. Everything politically, economically, morally, as well as in the religious-ecclesiastical sphere, is just as the prophecies of our Lord and of His

Apostles predict. The mystery of lawlessness is rushing to its predicted climax. The various "isms" of lawlessness, though differing from each other, are controlled by the spirit of atheism and antichristianity. The shadows of the masterpieces of Satan, the one who heads the political restored Roman Empire, and the other, the Antichrist, the man of sin, are lengthening. The politics of Europe are continually heading in the direction of what Daniel beheld in his visions. All is getting ready for the final years of the "Times of the Gentiles." Never has it been as dark in the world as it is now. In the Far East a war of horror sweeps hundreds of thousands away. What modern inventions of bombing planes, and various chemicals, and other destructive agencies can do is seen in the ruins of flourishing towns and cities of China. What will it be when the great conflict takes place in Europe? What will it be when the constantly increasing battle planes, loaded with thousands of tons of explosives begin their annihilating flights? Nor do we forget the internal strifes of nations, the revolution in Spain, the incipient revolutions among many nations, including the United States. "Distress of nations with perplexity," His holy lips predicted as a harbinger of His Coming again. It is all with us today. We refrain from mentioning again the falling away from the faith, the denials of all God is and God has made known by revelation to man, the rejection of Him, the Son of God, our Saviour-Lord, the sneers of infidels, including the apostates in various denominations, all written beforehand as a leading characteristic of the end of the age. Nor do we speak again of the plight of the Jews, the fast gathering clouds of their great tribulation.

What do these world conditions we have tabulated, with many more we might record, mean? True, it means a vindication, yes, a glorious vindication of the Bible as the supernatural Book of books. It means more than that. *It means the rapidly approaching realization of the hope of the Ages.* It means the coming of the Lord is at hand. But before His visible, personal and glorious appearing takes place, when He comes bringing His saints, the redeemed, with Him (1 Thess. iii:13), "that blessed hope" (Titus ii:13; 1 Thess. iv:16-18; 1 Cor. xv:51, 52; Phil. iii:21) must first come to pass. The events of the closing years of the "Times of the Gentiles," such as the complete apostasy, the mani- festation of the great dictator, the little horn (Dan. vii), as well as the final Antichrist, the full revival of the Roman Empire, the calling and sealing of the elect Israelitish remnant (Rev. vii) and other events, cannot come to pass till the Lord has fulfilled His promise given unto His own, and not to the world, "I will come again and receive you unto Myself, that where I am ye may be also." (John xiv:3). These events will not pass into history till His gracious prayer is answered, "Father, I will that they also, whom Thou hast given Me, be with Me where I am to behold My glory, which Thou hast given Me" (John xvii:24). The promised shout summoning the righteous dead from their graves, and the living believers to join them for the great face to face meeting in the air, will be the first great super- natural event which ushers in the final years of our age, heralding the fast approaching timed visible advent of the Son of man in great power and glory. It will be the final warning to the age. His coming for His saints will be fol- lowed by the great judgments and the outpouring of wrath so chronologically and vividly revealed in Revelation (chapters vi-xix).

How near is the realization of "that blessed hope"? As world conditions are ripe and ripening for the harvest, the end of the age, telling us of the nearness of the great reaper with His sharp sickle (Rev. xiv:14-16), His coming for the home gathering of the righteous, the beginning of the first resurrection must be *imminent*. And so it is. It is liable to occur at any time. The shout, the gathering shout, the welcoming shout which ends the waiting of Christ, the wait- ing of the Saints above and the waiting of Christ's true Church on earth, may soon be heard. We hear thousands answering—Amen! But better still we listen to His own words spoken from the glory. "Behold, I come quickly, hold that fast which thou hast, that no man take thy crown.

Him that overcometh will I make a pillar in the temple
of My God, and he shall no more go out; and I will write
upon him the name of My God, and the name of the city
of My God, which is new Jerusalem, which cometh down
out of heaven from My God; and I will write upon him My
new name" (Rev. iii:11-12). "Behold, I stand at the door,
and knock; if any man hear My voice, and open the door,
I will come in unto him, and will sup with him, and he with
Me. To him that overcometh will I grant to sit with Me
in My throne, even as I also overcame, and am set down
with My Father in His throne" (Rev. iii:20, 21). And here
His Spirit speaks, "Wherefore, beloved, seeing that ye look
for such things, be diligent that ye may be found of Him in
peace, without spot, and blameless" (2 Peter iii:14). "And
every man that hath this hope in Him purifieth himself,
even as He is pure" (1 John iii:3). "For yet a little while
and He that shall come will come and will not tarry" (Heb.
x:37). "Now unto Him that is able to keep you from stumbling, and to present you faultless before the presence of His
glory with exceeding joy, to the only wise God our Saviour,
be glory and majesty, dominion and power, both now and
for ever. Amen." (Jude, verses 24-25).

We will send to those who request it our full Book Catalog, Bible Reference Catalog and a free sample of OUR HOPE.